LANDLORD/TENANT RIGHTS
IN OREGON

LANDLORD/TENANT RIGHTS IN OREGON

Janay Ann Haas, Attorney

Self-Counsel Press Inc.
(a subsidiary of)
International Self-Counsel Press Ltd.
USA   Canada

Printed in Canada
First edition: 1978
Second edition: 1980
Third edition: 1988
Fourth edition: 1992
Fifth edition: 1994
Sixth edition: 1997
Seventh edition: 2004

National Library of Canada Cataloguing in Publication

Haas, Janay Ann
    Landlord/tenant rights in Oregon / Janay Ann Haas. — 7th ed.

(Self-counsel legal series)
Previous eds. by: Michael H. Marcus.

First ed. published under title: Landlord/tenant relations for Oregon.
ISBN 1-55180-429-8

1. Landlord and tenant—Oregon—Popular works. I. Marcus, Michael, 1943- II. Title. III. Series.
KFO2517.Z9M37 2004   346.79504'34   C2003-907358-0

Self-Counsel Press Inc.
(a subsidiary of)
International Self-Counsel Press Ltd.

1704 N. State Street	1481 Charlotte Road
Bellingham, WA 98225	North Vancouver, BC V7J 1H1
USA	Canada

*The author wishes to thank the Hon. Michael H. Marcus,
author of earlier editions of this book, and to thank attorneys
John Van Landingham and Edward Johnson for their assistance.*

CONTENTS

Tables

Samples

NOTICE

Laws are constantly changing. Every effort is made to keep this publication as current as possible. However, the author, the publisher, and the vendor make no representation or warranties regarding the outcome or the use to which the information in this book is put and are not assuming any liability for any claims, losses, or damages arising out of the use of this book. The reader should not rely on the author or publisher of this book for any professional advice. Please be sure you have the most recent edition.

INTRODUCTION

It's possible — although not advisable — to be a landlord* or a tenant for a long time without looking at Oregon's laws about your rights and duties. But when a problem arises, the question "What are my rights?" suddenly becomes important. By the time you ask the question, you may have already inadvertently given up some of those rights or stepped on someone else's. You may even be looking at an expensive trip to the courthouse.

This book aims to help you prevent problems in landlord-tenant relationships. It will explain the basic duties landlords and tenants owe each other, answer common questions, and offer practical solutions to real-life problems. This book will also show you how to create records of problems that may end up in court, which will help you be prepared if you need to prove your side of the story.

Although this book should help you solve problems without having to file or respond to a lawsuit, some cases do end up in court. If you think your situation might be one of them, don't assume you can safely handle the case yourself. The technical aspects of putting together a case can be complicated, so enlisting the help

---

*The word "landlord" in this book should be read to include the feminine "landlady."

of a lawyer can make the difference between success and failure. A small difference in facts can mean a big difference in the outcome of a case. Furthermore, if it is an eviction case, you should know that Oregon law provides for some of the fastest evictions in the nation. That means that whether you are a landlord or a tenant, if you think your case is headed for court, you should get some help from a lawyer as quickly as you can. If you do hire a lawyer, what you learn from this book may help you to prepare your side of the case and it may also help the person who is going to represent you.

CHAPTER ONE

OREGON'S RESIDENTIAL LANDLORD AND TENANT ACT

1. The Origins of the Law

Many misunderstandings between landlords and tenants arise because of mistaken beliefs about what the law requires. Some of those beliefs reflect what the law used to be in Oregon decades ago, before Oregon passed its Residential Landlord and Tenant Act. An understanding of how and why the law has changed is helpful to understanding the policy behind current law.

Landlord-tenant law in this country originally adopted old English legal principles. Historically, English landowners provided only bare land to tenants. The tenants provided their own shelter and paid rent in the form of crops and occasional military service for the landlord. If the crop failed, the tenant was sent packing and the landlord got back the land little the worse for wear and tear.

In the last two centuries, the role of the parties has changed. Landlords now provide the housing itself and tenants pay cash for the shelter provided by the landlord.

As housing construction and maintenance became increasingly complex, tenants could no longer be expected to have the skill or the money to make repairs to their units. Some landlords continued to apply the old rules, however, leaving responsibility for upkeep to the tenants. This practice led to acute problems in some urban areas where the inability of tenants to maintain units resulted in slum conditions. In response, more and more communities concluded that landlords, because of their superior expertise and financial condition, should assume responsibility for maintaining basic health and safety standards in residential rental units.

This gradual change in public policy was articulated in a model statute called the Uniform Residential Landlord and Tenant Act, which Oregon adopted with some changes in 1973. The law is now contained in Chapter 90 of the Oregon Revised Statutes (ORS). The Oregon Residential Landlord and Tenant Act (ORLTA) gives tenants rights to force landlords to make certain repairs and limits the power of landlords to evict tenants who exercise those rights.

Probably the hardest point for landlords to accept is that the law is intended to enforce basic housing standards for the benefit of the public as well as for the landlord and the tenant. It is easy to see that faulty sewage and plumbing systems can sicken many besides the tenant of a particular unit; that electrical and other fire hazards can put whole neighborhoods at risk; and that accumulating garbage can attract dangerous rodents and other vermin, resulting in widespread disease. Lawmakers wrestling with the issue of how best to protect public health and safety decided that tenants affected by poor housing conditions would be a cheaper law enforcement mechanism than large code-enforcement bureaucracies funded by tax dollars. Thus, a tenant who can't pay the rent but who has had to endure conditions that violate ORLTA can raise those problems as a defense to an eviction. If the problems are serious and the landlord knew or should have known of them, the tenant may very well get to stay in spite of being behind on the rent.

2. Who is Covered by the Act?

ORLTA and this book apply only to residential tenancies. The law covers all arrangements between someone who seems reasonably authorized to rent a unit and a tenant (including a tenant under age 18), so long as the premises are to be used for the tenant's home or residence. When the law applies, it gives tenants the rights of "exclusive possession" and "quiet enjoyment" of the property (see section 3.2 for more information), as well as certain other rights outlined below.

The law covers rooms, apartments and houses (both privately and publicly owned), mobile homes, floating homes, and other manufactured housing if their owners rent space for the home. Throughout this book, some of the rights described may be somewhat different in manufactured housing and floating home facilities (see chapter 13 for more specific information). Neither the residential law nor this book applies to commercial or business tenancies, and the laws about those kinds of tenancies do not apply to residential tenancies.

ORLTA *does* apply if —

(a) the tenancy is not excluded by ORS 90.110, and

(b) there is some form of understanding between —

    (i) a "landlord" (the owner, lessor, sublessor, manager, or, in some situations, someone who has the authority to act on behalf of a landlord); and

    (ii) a person entitled because of that understanding to occupy a residence or sleeping place.

The coverage of the law is broad, to carry out the public policy described above, but ORS 90.110 excludes the following kinds of occupancies from coverage:

(a) Occupants of institutional residences, such as detention homes, nursing care facilities, and school dormitories

(b) Transient occupants of hotels, motels, and users of vacation rentals

(c) Landlords' employees whose occupancy is conditional on employment in and about the premises (although housing for farm workers provides protection from eviction; see chapters 8 and 14)

(d) Condominium owners

(e) Members of cooperatives

(f) Those who rent primarily for agricultural purposes

(g) Buyers occupying premises they are purchasing under a contract of sale, and sellers occupying a place they have just sold, for no more than 90 days before or after the sale closes, and only if the sale agreement allows for it

(h) Members of fraternal organizations in buildings operated for the benefit of the organizations

(i) Trespassers and "squatters"

Not everyone who stays in hotels or motels is denied protections by the ORLTA. ORS 90.100(44) says that an occupant is "transient" only if all the following criteria apply:

(a) Occupancy charges must be charged on a daily basis and payable no more than six days in advance.

(b) The management must provide maid and linen service daily or every two days.

(c) The period of occupancy must not exceed 30 days. The landlord cannot keep an occupant from becoming a tenant by changing the person's room every 30 days.

"Vacation occupancy" is the rental of a dwelling unit for vacation purposes when the occupant has a principal home elsewhere and when the agreed-upon stay is for no more than 45 days.

A landlord cannot avoid the application of the law by making creative arrangements: the courts will look at the real nature of the relationship. ORLTA specifically points out one such arrangement as improper: a tenant who lives in a rental with an option to purchase remains a tenant until the option is exercised (ORS 90.110).

Despite these definitions, it can be difficult to decide whether your situation is covered by ORLTA. A knowledgeable lawyer may be able to help you determine the scope of your rights.

3. What Are the Landlord's Obligations?

3.1 Habitability

ORS 90.320 requires landlords to maintain habitable premises at all times during the tenancy. Habitability requirements include the following:

(a) Plumbing, heating, and electrical systems that conform to applicable law when installed and must be maintained in good working order

(b) Effective waterproofing and weather protection

(c) A water supply approved under applicable law, which can be controlled by the tenant or the landlord. The water supply must be capable of producing hot and cold running water, be furnished to appropriate fixtures, and connected to a legally approved sewage disposal system, maintained so as to produce safe drinking water, and kept in good working order to the extent that the system can be controlled by the landlord.

(d) Floors, walls, ceilings, stairways, and railings in good repair

(e) Ventilation, air conditioning, and other appliances (including elevators) in good repair, if supplied by the landlord

(f) Working smoke detectors and safety from fire hazards (Landlords are responsible for maintaining and testing smoke detectors in common areas.)

(g) Working locks for all outside doors and keys for any locks requiring them, and latches for windows as permitted by law. (**Note:** Some tenants who are victims of stalking, domestic violence, or sexual assault crimes have the right to change these at their own expense. See *2003 Oregon Laws*, chapter 378, and chapters 10 and 14 of this book.)

(h) At the beginning of the tenancy, the building and grounds must be safe for normal and reasonable uses. They must be clean; sanitary; and free from accumulations of debris, filth, rubbish, garbage, rodents, and vermin. Thereafter, all areas under the control of the landlord must be kept in these safe and clean conditions.

(i) At the beginning of the tenancy, the landlord must provide an adequate number of trash containers, unless the landlord and tenant have a written agreement to deal with disposal some other way or unless local law has different requirements. The containers must be clean and in good repair, and the landlord must continue to provide and maintain them throughout the tenancy.

Some cities and counties may require landlords to make recycling containers available for tenants. ORS 90.318 describes the duties of landlords in cities with multifamily recycling service. These landlords, if they have at least five units at one location, must provide up to four containers for materials accepted in the curbside recycling program, arrange for collection services, and notify new tenants (and then, annually, existing tenants) of how to use the containers and where to find them.

ORLTA does not allow a landlord to get a tenant to waive the right to a safe, decent place to live (ORS 90.135, 90.245, 90.320). The general rule is that responsibility for maintaining habitability belongs only to the landlord, with one narrow exception. ORS 90.145 permits a landlord to enter into an agreement with a tenant or a tenant-to-be to make repairs, do routine maintenance, and clean in the person's own unit in exchange for a reduction in rent. (This kind of agreement isn't an option for tenants who want to get paid to clean up their own messes.) The tenant may not do electrical or plumbing work unless licensed to do so. ORS 90.320 also allows for written agreements with tenants to perform specific repairs or minor remodeling only if the landlord pays the tenant for the work and the agreement does not shift the responsibility for habitability from the landlord to the tenant. For example, the landlord and a tenant could agree that the tenant would paint the tenant's unit for money, or in lieu of a security deposit, or some other kind of reimbursement.

No landlord, of course, is responsible for maintaining a manufactured home owned by a tenant, although a landlord may be liable for damage to the tenant's home caused by the landlord's failure to maintain safe conditions on the land or moorage where the unit sits. Tenants in manufactured housing facilities also have a duty to keep their units safe to prevent harm to others in the facility.

3.2 Tenant's privacy

The law gives the tenant the right to "exclusive possession" of the rental (in other words, privacy) against intrusion by or at the direction of the landlord (ORS 90.322). This right of privacy extends to all parts of the rental property in which the tenant has exclusive control (for example, the yard of a single-family rental unless the landlord has — in a written rental agreement — taken on the responsibility of yard maintenance). The right of privacy does not extend to areas used by others, such as halls and stairwells in multifamily buildings. Landlords can enter a tenant's unit only with a court order or unless one of the following circumstances applies:

(a) The tenants have abandoned the premises. (The tenants have left under circumstances clearly demonstrating that they have no intention of returning.)

(b) The tenants have relinquished the premises. (They have expressly or implicitly given up possession of the premises for good.)

(c) The tenants have been absent for more than seven days and entry is necessary for a reasonable purpose.

(d) The landlord is entering the premises (but not the dwelling unit itself) to serve notices required or permitted under the rental agreement, ORLTA, or other applicable law.

(e) There is an emergency, such as a repair problem that is likely to cause serious damage to the premises if not addressed immediately. After this kind of entry, the landlord must let the tenant know within the following 24 hours the date and time of the entry, the emergency that required entry, and the identities of those who entered.

(f) The tenant has asked in writing for the landlord to enter to make repairs. In this case, the tenant authorizes the landlord to enter to make those repairs at the times specified in the request or, if the tenant doesn't specify times, at any reasonable time. After a written request for repair, a landlord may enter on demand, in the tenant's absence and without consent, until the repairs are complete. The authority to enter expires automatically after seven days from the request unless repairs are in progress and the landlord is making a reasonable effort to complete them in a timely manner. Any worker other than the landlord should be prepared to show written evidence of his or her authority to make the repair if the tenant asks for proof.

(g) The landlord has given the tenant at least 24 hours' actual notice of intent to enter, so long as the entry is at a reasonable time and for a reasonable purpose. ("Actual notice" can be made verbally in person, by fax, by phone, or on an answering machine or can be made in writing, delivered personally or left secured to the main entrance at the residential address.)

Reasonable purposes include inspections, repairs, decorations, alterations, improvements, necessary or agreed-on services, or showing of the unit to buyers or potential buyers, tenants, workers, contractors, and mortgagees.

(h) The landlord or agent of the landlord is entering to show the premises for sale after the landlord and tenant have signed a valid agreement permitting such entries. Because property buyers are not likely to await the tenant's convenience to see a property for sale, the landlord and tenant can make an independent agreement for entry for this purpose, provided the property is actively on the market at the time and provided that the landlord gives the tenant fair compensation for the inconvenience. This agreement cannot be part of the rental agreement itself. If the tenancy is month to month, the compensation may simply be that the landlord is giving up the right to evict without cause. In tenancies that require cause to evict (and that do not reserve the right to terminate because the landlord wants to show the premises for sale), the landlord may have to reduce the rent or give the tenant something else of value to make the agreement enforceable.

There are some additional limitations on the exceptions above. For example, it is unlawful for a landlord to attempt to make the tenant waive privacy rights in the rental agreement (ORS 90.245).

Landlords cannot abuse the right of access or use it to harass tenants. Landlords who abuse their access right are subject to damages and injunctions. They may not enter if tenants do not consent, but landlords have a remedy in court against tenants who deny access unreasonably. In addition, if a government agency requires access to any part of the premises under the tenant's control and the landlord is unable to get in after following this part of ORLTA, the government cannot hold the landlord liable for being unable to gain entry.

Landlords of mobile homes, recreational vehicles used as homes, manufactured housing, and floating homes where the landlords do not own the housing may enter a rented space only for the purposes of normal maintenance and the posting of legally-required notices.

3.3 The duty of owners or managers to identify themselves

The person who enters into the rental agreement on behalf of the landlord must disclose to the tenant, in writing, at or before the beginning of the tenancy, the name and address of the person authorized to manage the premises and the name and address of an owner or person authorized to act for the owner for the purposes of receiving and giving receipts for notices and demands. If that person does not give out this information, everyone who is authorized by the landlord to manage or enter into rental agreements will be treated as an agent of the landlord (ORS 90.305).

This information must be kept current. If new owners or managers do not keep the information current and the tenant contacts the prior landlord in good faith, the new landlord is treated as having received the contact.

3.4 The duty of landlords to disclose

Under the federal Lead Paint Disclosure Act of 1992, landlords of properties built before 1978 must warn prospective tenants of the possibility of harm from exposure to lead-based paint that may have been used on the property. This law applies not only to owners, but also to their agents and to realtors. Except in certain circumstances (described below), they must —

(a) provide the tenant with a copy of Protect Your Family from Lead in Your Home, an Environmental Protection Agency pamphlet available from the National Lead Information Center at 1-800-424-LEAD;

(b) disclose to the tenant the existence and location of any lead-based paint and paint hazards, the basis for the belief that lead-based paint or lead-based paint hazards are present, and the condition of painted surfaces;

(c) provide the tenant with available records and reports about the lead-based paint or hazards on the property (In multifamily housing, records and reports about common-area paint or hazards must be disclosed. In some cases, conditions in other units must also be disclosed.); and

(d) do all of the above before entering into the rental agreement, giving the prospective tenant an opportunity to review the information.

Rental agreements must include a lead warning and tenant acknowledgment (see Sample 1). Landlords can find copies of the necessary forms, along with more detailed information, on the Web site <www.epa.gov/lead>.

Three types of housing are exempt from the lead-based paint disclosure law:

(a) Housing for households in which at least one person is 62 years old or older at the start of the tenancy

(b) Housing for individuals with disabilities (unless children younger than age 6 live, or are expected to live, there also)

SAMPLE 1
LEAD WARNING STATEMENT

Sample Disclosure Format for Target Housing Rentals and Leases
Disclosure of Information on Lead-Based Paint and Lead-Based Paint Hazards

Lead Warning Statement
Housing built before 1978 may contain lead-based paint. Lead from paint, paint chips, and dust can pose health hazards if not taken care of properly. Lead exposure is especially harmful to young children and pregnant women. Before renting pre-1978 housing, landlords must disclose the presence of known lead-based paint and lead-based paint hazards in the dwelling. Tenants must also receive a Federally approved pamphlet on lead poisoning prevention.

Lessor's Disclosure (initial)

_____ (a)   Presence of lead-based paint or lead-based paint hazards (check one below):

☐ Known lead-based paint and/or lead-based paint hazards are present in the housing (explain).

_____

_____

☐ Lessor has no knowledge of lead-based paint and/or lead-based paint hazards in the housing.

_____ (b)   Records and reports available to the lessor (check one below):

☐ Lessor has provided the lessee with all available records and reports pertaining to lead-based paint and/or lead-based paint hazards in the housing (list documents below).

_____

_____

☐ Lessor has no reports or records pertaining to lead-based paint and/or lead-based paint hazards in the housing.

Lessee's Acknowledgment (initial)
_____ (c)   Lessee has received copies of all information listed above.
_____ (d)   Lessee has received the pamphlet *Protect Your Family from Lead in Your Home.*

Agent's Acknowledgment (initial)
_____ (e)   Agent has informed the lessor of the lessor's obligations under 42 U.S.C. 4582(d) and is aware of his/her responsibility to ensure compliance.

Certification of Accuracy
The following parties have reviewed the information above and certify, to the best of their knowledge, that the information provided by the signatory is true and accurate.

Lessor	Date	Lessor	Date
Lessee	Date	Lessee	Date
Agent	Date	Agent	Date

(c) Units such as studio apartments, barracks, and dormitories where the living and sleeping areas are not separate

There are four types of transactions that are also exempt from the law:

(a) Sales on foreclosure

(b) Housing that has been certified to be free of lead-based paint by an accredited inspector

(c) Renewals of existing leases after a landlord has already disclosed and has no new information

(d) Closed-term, nonrenewable leases of 100 or fewer days

For existing tenants, the landlord's duty to disclose arises when there is any significant change in rent amount or other lease terms.

If the premises in which the dwelling unit is located contain no more than four dwelling units, the landlord must notify the tenant when the rental agreement is to be executed (i.e., soon enough so the tenant can decide not to rent) if the premises are subject to —

(a) an outstanding notice of default under a trust deed or a trustee's sale;

(b) a pending suit to foreclose a mortgage, trust deed, or vendor's lien under a contract of sale;

(c) a pending declaration of forfeiture or suit for specific performance of a contract of sale; or

(d) a pending proceeding to foreclose a tax lien.

A tenant who has to move as a result of a circumstance the landlord failed to disclose is entitled to twice the actual damages or twice the monthly rent, whichever is greater, and all prepaid rent. "Actual damages" include moving expenses if the tenant can demonstrate that they were caused by the landlord's omission. In other words, a tenant who decides to move across the country won't get moving expenses, even if the move was the result of a proceeding the landlord should have told the tenant about when the rental agreement was being negotiated (ORS 90.310).

As a practical matter, a tenant may be unsuccessful in getting any satisfaction from a landlord in this situation even if the tenant gets a judgment against the landlord in court. A landlord in such serious financial straits that a foreclosure is underway may have little left for the tenant to take in compensation.

These disclosure obligations don't affect a court-appointed receiver or a manager who has complied with the disclosure requirements listed in the last section and who was ignorant of the circumstance that should have been disclosed. The remedies run against the landlord who should have told the manager to tell the tenant instead of against both the manager and the landlord.

Landlords also must disclose, in writing at or before the beginning of the tenancy, any utility or service for which the tenant pays directly to a provider and which directly benefits the landlord or other tenants (ORS 90.315).

4. What Are the Tenant's Obligations?

This may seem obvious, but tenants can occupy a residential unit only as a residence, unless the parties agree otherwise (and if zoning laws permit additional uses) (ORS 90.340).

Under ORS 90.325, tenants must use all portions of the premises and all facilities and appliances "reasonably." Tenants are also responsible for —

- keeping the areas under their control as clean, sanitary, and free of trash as the condition of the premises permits;

- removing rodents or other vermin they have brought or encouraged to come onto the property;

- cooperating with landlords' reasonable efforts to fix problems at the property; and

- disposing of waste in a clean, safe, and lawful manner. In the case of needles, syringes, and other infectious waste, that means following specific state health and safety laws (ORS 459.386).

- paying required fees and deposits.

The following three duties are also required by tenants (and can become complicated in a tenancy involving roommates):

- Tenants must pay agreed-on rent when it is due.

- Tenants must not damage, deliberately or accidentally, any part of the premises.

- Tenants must not disturb their neighbors. This duty includes controlling the behavior of guests.

What do the paying roommates do if one roommate stops paying? What if the tenants have a lease and one of them moves out before the lease period ends? What happens if one of the roommates moves out and the remaining tenants can't afford the rent? What is the liability of conscientious roommates for a co-tenant who damages the rental or has rowdy parties or out-of-control visitors? While most tenants might feel more secure having separate rental agreements when they have roommates, most landlords are not interested in becoming involved in squabbles regarding which of the roommates should be evicted because of a string of disturbances or who is responsible for which portion of the rent. Landlords will prefer one rental agreement that makes each cosignor fully responsible for carrying out that agreement.

Tenants may not unreasonably deny access to the rental by the landlord after the landlord has given reasonable notice and has a legitimate reason to enter (ORS 90.322). Tenants must test battery-operated smoke detectors provided by the landlord according to the manufacturer's instructions at least every six months. They are responsible for replacing batteries once the set provided by the landlord no longer works. If the smoke alarm doesn't work properly, a tenant can hold the landlord liable for fire damage only after giving the landlord written notice that the alarm is defective. Tenants may not remove or tamper with a working smoke detector and may not remove working batteries.

Rental agreements can impose other requirements on tenants. For example, they can require the tenant to give actual notice to the landlord of any expected absence of more than seven days no later than the first day of that absence (ORS 90.340).

All tenants have a duty under the law to notify landlords of habitability problems (to prevent the problem's getting worse and more expensive to repair) and of their intention to move. (See chapter 10 for details).

CHAPTER TWO

STARTING A TENANCY

1. What Tenants Should Know about Landlords

A key time for both landlords and tenants to avoid trouble is before the tenancy starts. No tenant wants to pay good money to live in unreasonable conditions, and no landlord wants to risk the safety and quality of a rental unit on someone who won't care for or pay for the unit.

Most tenants don't have the luxury of finding a "perfect" landlord. But with some advance inquiry, they can minimize their risk. One of the best ways to find out about the landlord is to ask current tenants in other rentals owned by the same landlord. The tax assessor in your county can tell you where the owner has properties there. You can look at those properties to see if they are well maintained. You also can learn about your prospective landlord at the court clerk's office at the county courthouse. There you can discover how often the landlord has sued tenants in eviction cases, what kinds of defenses the tenants raised in those cases, and whether the tenants or the landlord won the case. If you see numerous cases in which tenants claimed the landlord refused to make requested repairs or tenants were evicted in retaliation because they asked for repairs, you are probably looking at a landlord you want to avoid. You can also see how often tenants have taken the landlord to small claims court to try to get their deposits back after they have moved out. Sometimes city or county building inspectors can tell you whether your landlord has been cited for allowing rentals to violate health and safety code standards.

Your can also look at a Web site, <www.apartmentratings.com> for tenant reviews of places throughout Oregon.

2. How Should a Landlord Screen Tenants?

Screening tenants has become both an art and a science. To demonstrate compliance with the federal Fair Housing Act and various state and local laws, landlords are required to select tenants objectively and must be able to justify their selection. They must not discriminate against families with children, racial and ethnic minorities, or individuals with physical or mental handicaps, among other criteria. Similar state laws prohibit discrimination based on source of income, past successful defenses against eviction, or status as the victim of domestic violence, sexual assault, or stalking. Some local ordinances prohibit discrimination on the basis of sexual orientation, age, and gender identity (see chapter 14).

You should be familiar with anti-discrimination laws, but you should also recognize that it is not illegal to discriminate on the basis of employment history, criminal history, or rental history. Most practical of all, you do have the right to discriminate on the basis of disparity between disclosed income and apparent means. For example, if an applicant is on welfare but drives a new luxury car, ask how this is possible and do not fear the law if you refuse the rental based on an incredible or unverifiable response. If you rent to tenants who are members of protected classes (i.e., those groups mentioned in the anti-discrimination laws), if your screening policy is directly related to the tenancy itself, and if you apply your screening criteria to all applicants equally, you should not get into trouble with the law if you reject, for a good and lawful reason, an applicant who happens to be a member of a protected class.

Some landlords require tenants to demonstrate an income that is twice or three times the amount of the rent. Such a policy may be unlawfully discriminatory. Furthermore, landlords are discovering that the amount of income doesn't seem to predict the tenant's ability to pay the rent. As a result, several very large Oregon landlords have abandoned this "three times the rent" policy in recent years. There's not much point in using such a standard if it doesn't improve your ability to get and retain good tenants, especially if it exposes you to potential liability.

You must be vigilant about "drug houses" and "meth labs." A tenant who sells or manufactures drugs can get you into a lot of trouble as a result of criminal forfeiture laws that theoretically threaten your ownership or continued operation of a rental property if it has been used for such purposes. (This hazard also includes prostitution or gambling.) A rental unit used as a drug manufacturing plant can be so toxic that certified professional cleaners must be hired to make the unit legally safe for occupancy. It is often cheaper to tear down the unit than to restore it to the market. Other tenants suffer even more than the property owner because their quality of life and safety are most directly threatened by a neighboring tenant's drug activities.

The National Institute of Justice offers helpful tips for landlords in J. H. Campbell's *Landlord Training Program: Keeping Illegal Activity out of Rental Property* (publication #133278). Although the booklet's information about Oregon's landlord-tenant law is not current, its tips about monitoring for drug activity are excellent. Look for more information at the National Criminal Justice Reference Service's Web site <www.ncjrs.org>.

It is essential to check employment and prior landlord references intelligently and meticulously. Get phone numbers from the telephone book, not from the tenant-applicant, and call. Verify that a prior landlord is really that, and not a friend who agreed to provide the tenant with a sham reference. A criminal background check is a good idea, too. Several landlord associations offer screening services for landlords who do not want to do the screening themselves.

Owners should do even more screening of managers. A poor choice may haunt you in many costly ways, not least in poor tenant screening. Owners can be personally liable for the actions of their managers. Oregon law now requires that certain categories of property managers be trained and licensed. Check with the Oregon Board of Realty or a competent attorney familiar with the requirements to see if your manager needs to be licensed.

2.1 Applicant screening charges, tenant screening services, and credit reporting agencies

You may charge for screening before accepting a tenant (ORS 90.295). The charge is to cover your expenses in obtaining information on the prospective tenant, such as the cost of a credit reporting agency or tenant screening service. The charge cannot be greater than your average actual cost of screening applicants, including the reasonable value of time spent by you or your employees in obtaining information. Nor can it be greater than the customary amount charged by tenant screening services or consumer credit agencies for a comparable level of screening.

To charge for applicant screening, you must have written screening or admission criteria, and you must notify the applicant in advance and in writing of —

(a) what a tenant screening or consumer credit report entails and what you will charge for it, and

(b) the right to dispute the accuracy of any information provided by a screening or credit reporting service.

You must give the applicant a receipt for the application charge. You must refund the money within a reasonable time if for any reason you do not actually screen the applicant or you fill the vacant unit before screening the applicant.

Whether or not you charge an applicant screening fee, if you reject an applicant in whole or in part because of a tenant screening or credit report, you must notify the applicant of that fact at the same time you notify the applicant of the rejection. You must give the applicant the name and address of the reporting or screening service in writing. You may provide the applicant with a copy of the report, but you are not required to disclose the contents of any report other than a consumer report subject to the Fair Credit Reporting Act.

Unless the applicant agrees otherwise in writing, you may not charge for applicant screening when you know or should know that no units are available or will be available within a reasonable time. Thus, you may not charge an applicant for the privilege of getting onto a waiting list. If you violate any of these provisions relating to applicant screening fees, the applicant may recover the amount of the fee plus $100.

Landlords have the right to ask for a deposit to hold a unit for a prospective tenant for a period of time the parties agree on (ORS 90.140). If you and the applicant then enter the rental agreement, you must either apply the deposit to the amount owed by the tenant under the rental agreement (as part of the first month's rent) or refund it to the tenant immediately. If the applicant decides not to rent the unit after all, you may keep the deposit as damages. If you change your mind about renting to the applicant after you have accepted a deposit to hold the place, you must return the deposit to the applicant within four days.

2.2 What about tenant "blacklisting" services?

There are several tenant-screening services that sell information about tenants to landlords who want a quick way to predict whether applicants are a good risk. These services vary in their responsibility, accuracy, and the extent of information they provide. (Landlords also vary in what they consider to be disqualifying information. It is unlawful to reject a tenant on grounds that the tenant won an eviction case on the merits against a past landlord [ORS 90.390].)

These services usually check court records of evictions (the records are public information) and simply keep a list of all tenants named as eviction defendants. Some services stop there; the better ones follow the cases and remove the names of tenants whose cases were dismissed or who won the case. Some merely supplement the information when these things happen, but retain the names on the list. The most responsible services remove the names in these cases and rely on other sources of information as well.

The Fair Credit Reporting Act, a federal statute, gives consumers some protection in these cases.

The tenant applicant whose name is on a "blacklist" has the following rights:

(a) A landlord who relies on a tenant screening service's information to reject a tenant must tell the tenant the source of any information subject to disclosure under the Fair Credit Reporting Act.

(b) The tenant can demand to see the information the service has.

(c) The tenant can demand that the service reinvestigate and correct any wrong information about the tenant, and insist that the tenant's side of the dispute be set forth in future disclosures.

The federal law has statutory penalties for sellers and users of such services who do not honor these rights. A tenant may be able to get the record corrected to show he or she won, not lost, an eviction case.

Tenants who have problems with a tenant screening service — especially if they have reason to believe the information being given out is incorrect and making it hard for them to find a place to live — should try to remedy the situation with telephone calls and letters to the service citing the Fair Credit Reporting Act. Some services are quite conscientious in responding to legitimate requests and will correct mistakes, even taking a tenant's name off the list if necessary. If the service does not cooperate, tenants should contact the Oregon attorney general's consumer division or find an attorney familiar with consumers' rights (see chapter 15).

CHAPTER THREE

ENTERING INTO A RENTAL AGREEMENT

1. Finding a Home

1.1 Tenants: What can you afford?

If you haven't looked for a place to live lately, you may be shocked to learn that, nationwide, rents have shot up by a third over the last five years. Couple that with the knowledge that the inability to pay rent is the most common reason tenants in Oregon are evicted, and you can conclude how important it is to evaluate your needs and resources before deciding where and what to rent.

The cost of renting a home includes not only the rent itself, but also the cost of utilities the tenant has to pay, fees and deposits, and other factors. For example, if you don't have reliable transportation, it's a bad idea to rent that "dream place" out in the country if there is no other way to get to work in town. For another example, if you move into a poorly insulated home because the rent is cheap, you may have to move again when you get your winter heat bills.

Do you have appliances? If not, can you buy new or used appliances for an amount that would make living in a place without them more economical than living in a place that costs more because the landlord supplies the appliances? If you have no clothes washer or dryer, is there access to a convenient laundry service? If not, is the purchase of a washer going to be part of the cost of moving into a particular place? Does that place have the necessary electrical and plumbing hookups to allow you to use one if you buy it? If you rent a place with housemates, how long can you afford to stay in the place on your own if they move out? What about the cost of parking and car insurance or public transportation in some of Oregon's urban areas?

More and more landlords require first and last months' rent, deposits and, in some cases, fees, so you should calculate the maximum amount of those expenses that your budget can withstand. Once you have a clear picture of the actual costs entailed in renting a particular unit in a particular neighborhood, you can enter into a rental agreement with more confidence.

1.2   How do you begin the search?

In the search for housing, the two most important rules are to allow as much time as possible and to prepare for disappointments. Otherwise, you will be more likely to take a place you're not really happy with just to free yourself from the agony of the search.

The best way to find a place is through a friend who is moving or who knows someone who is. The friend can tell you what you need to know about the place, the landlord, and the neighborhood.

Look at newspaper classified ads, signs on store bulletin boards, and other free sources of similar listings in your community. If there's a trick to this process, it is to get up early and chase down the new ads as soon as you can; good deals go fast in most rental markets.

If you are looking at obviously run-down housing, there are two more places you might want to check: the building inspector and the police. The inspector's office should be able to tell you whether the rental has been posted with a notice as "unlawful to occupy." Sometimes a dishonest landlord will simply rip the notice off the building and rent to desperate tenants. The police may be able to tell you whether a suspiciously vacant rental was a "drug house," which may pose a health hazard.

1.3 Why avoid agencies?

Services that give prospective tenants access to listings for a fee are a last resort. Theoretically, these services keep their listings current and promptly remove rentals that are no longer available. Several years ago, an Oregon State Public Interest Research Group (OSPIRG) research project concluded that these agencies often maintain obsolete listings. Such agencies continue to exist, however, and some people do find satisfactory housing through them.

2. Making a Deal

Once you have found a place or are seriously interested in one, the next step is to make a deal. Assuming you haven't encountered a hard-line "take it or leave it" landlord, it's surprising how much can be negotiated to your advantage without costing the landlord anything.

2.1 Requirements of a rental agreement

What is a rental agreement, anyway? A valid rental agreement is a legally binding contract — oral or written — between the landlord and the tenant. It lays out the duties and expectations of both parties. Before landlords enter into an agreement, it's a good idea for them to get some legal advice about the terms they want to impose on the tenants. Tenants need to understand the agreement, too.

Whether the agreement is written or oral, all rental agreements have to meet certain legal requirements:

(a) If the agreement is in writing, the landlord must give a copy to the tenant (ORS 90.240).

(b) The landlord must identify in writing an owner and a manager, if there is one, and provide an address for getting in touch. The landlord must update the information for the tenant when there is a change (ORS 90.305).

(c) The landlord must notify the tenant in writing if any utility paid for directly by the tenant benefits the landlord or other tenants (ORS 90.315). If the tenant must pay the landlord directly for other utilities and services (cable, heat, Internet access, trash collection, etc.), this information must appear in a written rental agreement.

(d) The tenant is bound by the landlord's rules, in addition to those in any rental agreement (ORS 90.262), but only if —

   (i)   the tenant has written notice of the rule when entering the rental agreement or when the rule is adopted;

   (ii)   the purpose of the rule is to promote the convenience, safety, or welfare of tenants; to protect the landlord's property; or to distribute services and facilities among tenants fairly;

   (iii)   the rule is reasonably related to its purpose;

   (iv)   the rule applies to all tenants in a fair manner;

   (v)   the rule is clear and understandable;

   (vi)   the rule is not designed to enable the landlord to evade his or her obligations; and

   (vii)   if the rule is adopted after the tenant enters into the rental agreement and the rule creates a "substantial modification" of the tenant's rights, the tenant consents to the rule in writing. (Different laws about rules apply to mobile home parks and floating home facilities. See chapter 13.)

2.2 Types of rental agreements

Rental agreements generally fall into three categories: month-to-month tenancies; week-to-week tenancies; and "fixed-term" tenancies or leases. Somewhat different rules apply to each category.

If a rental agreement does not specify a fixed term, the tenancy is assumed to be a month-to-month tenancy (ORS 90.240). A month-to-month agreement may not require a tenant to forfeit deposits or rent if the tenant does not stay in the rental for a minimum period of time (ORS 90.300). If the tenancy is month-to-month, the rent is payable at the beginning of each monthly term. (Thus, if the first day of the tenancy falls on the fifteenth day of a month, the rent is payable on the fifteenth of each month.) Landlords must give 30 days' written notice if they plan to raise the rent on a month-to-month tenancy.

A rental agreement can be characterized as a week-to-week or vacation-home tenancy if it meets all of the requirements for those exceptions. Landlords must give seven days' written notice on a week-to-week tenancy. On a fixed-term tenancy, the landlord cannot raise the rent without the tenant's agreement.

Note: Unless the tenant and landlord agree otherwise, the tenant can pay the rent at his or her dwelling unit.

2.3 Informal dispute resolution

It is lawful to include a provision in a rental agreement for informal dispute resolution. This provision can be helpful to both sides in preventing an expensive showdown in court later on. Many communities have free community mediation services the parties can use, although community programs that do not know about landlord-tenant laws may do a disservice by getting a tenant to "waive" rights that cannot be waived — such as the tenant's right to a place that is safe to live. A landlord cannot rely on such a waiver. Acting in good faith is a requirement of the law, too (ORS 90.100). The landlord who defines "informal dispute resolution" as a threatening letter from his or her lawyer is hardly observing the intent of the law.

2.4 Provisions a rental agreement cannot contain

There are several provisions a rental agreement must not contain (ORS 90.245). The following provisions are unenforceable if they appear in a rental agreement:

(a) Provisions that are "unconscionable" (These are provisions so one-sided, harsh, or shocking that a person would have to be desperate to agree to them.)

(b) Provisions designed to waive tenants' rights under the act

(c) Provisions that allow a landlord to get a court judgment without giving tenants an opportunity to appear and defend themselves

(d) Provisions that protect the landlord from liability for negligence or willful misconduct.

A court can refuse to enforce an unconscionable provision of a rental agreement (ORS 90.135). A landlord is liable to his or her tenant for up to three months' rent in addition to actual damages if he or she deliberately uses a rental agreement containing a provision described by (b), (c), or (d) of the list above; knows that the provision is prohibited; and attempts to enforce the provision. A landlord who enforces a forfeiture provision will be liable for twice the amount of money withheld.

2.5 Tenant's duties

The tenant has certain duties under any rental agreement, regardless of the length of the term or whether the agreement is written or oral (ORS 90.325). The tenant is responsible for the following duties:

(a) Reasonable use of the premises and appliances for their intended purposes

(b) Reasonable cleanliness, so as to avoid danger of fire, the infestation of rodents and bugs, etc.

(c) Proper disposal of medical and infectious waste

(d) Test smoke alarms or smoke detectors at least once every six months, replacement of detector batteries as needed, and not removing batteries or disconnecting a properly working alarm or detector

(e) Conduct by tenant and guests that does not disturb the peaceful enjoyment of other tenants or neighbors

(f) Payment of rent in advance of the rental period (seven days, 30 days, etc.)

The tenant and the landlord can agree in writing that the tenant can make rent payments in regular installments of less than a month under a schedule laid out in that agreement (ORS 90.415).

A rental agreement can also require a tenant to notify the landlord no later than the first day of an extended absence from the rental of more than seven days (ORS 90.340).

2.6 Promises concerning repairs and furnishings

It is common for landlords to promise at the beginning of a tenancy to perform specific repairs or to supply the tenant with items like paint, a stove, or a lawn mower. Tenants should not be afraid to ask that the promise — including the date by which the promise is to be performed — be put in writing. The back of the rent receipt will do if it is signed by the landlord or the landlord's agent. A landlord who is unwilling to put a promise in writing is probably unwilling to perform the promise. If the landlord refuses, carefully consider whether you want the place without the promised repair or supplies.

2.7 Limitations on rent hikes and eviction

If a tenant does not have a lease for a term of several months or a year or more, a landlord is usually free to evict the tenant without stating the reason or raise the rent after giving 30 days' notice (ORS 90.240). A clear exception exists when the tenant has paid several months' rent in advance. Another exception is the law for manufactured home facilities or mobile home parks (see chapter 13). Additional considerations apply when the tenant is on active military duty.

A tenant who expects to stay for a long time can ask the landlord to consider a one-year lease (or whatever term the tenant wants) rather than leave the agreement on a month-to-month basis. A landlord may be reluctant to sign a lease for fear that expenses will rise and reduce his or her profit, but a lease that incorporates the landlord's actual increases in taxes and specified operating expenses may be acceptable. Such clauses are common in commercial leases and generally function to the mutual advantage of both parties. Try to describe the cost increases that can result in an increase in rent as specifically as possible.

A landlord may be fearful of losing the power to evict a "bad" tenant. Again, ask for details of unacceptable behavior. Have previous tenants thrown loud parties or parked junk cars in the flower bed? Point out that a landlord always has the right to evict for nonpayment of rent, for material violations of a rental agreement, and for abuse of the property (see chapter 8), and that his or her power to evict for cause is not diminished by adding rules of conduct to a rental agreement for a term. For example, if the rental agreement says that no cars may be parked in the flower bed, the landlord can evict the tenant if the problem is not remedied or for repeated violations even if the tenant has a 50-year lease.

Sometimes it is the landlord who wants a lease; this practice is common where there are many empty rentals, and in communities with predictable population flows that can cause landlords to make less money. For example, a small town with a university may have a large number of vacancies in the summer; landlords in a town that attracts summer tourists willing to pay high prices for housing are likely to have 8- or 9-month long winter leases followed by an eviction notice or a dramatic rent hike in June.

3. Written versus Verbal Agreements

There are arguments for and against both written and verbal agreements, although as the discussion above indicates, the increasing complexity of the law means that written agreements are becoming more and more the standard. The Landlord and Tenant Act has included most of the provisions a tenant is likely to get in a rental agreement, and oral agreements are presumed to include those provisions.

3.1 Problems tenants can avoid with oral agreements

In a written agreement, the landlord may —

(a) shift, in exchange for fair payment, to the tenant the landlord's obligation to make certain minor repairs (**Note**: This shift does not make the tenant an employee of the landlord who would then not be subject to the law. Nor does it allow landlords to rent units lacking heat, adequate plumbing, safe water, or other habitability requirements even if the tenant signs an agreement. [ORS 90.145].);

(b) escape liability for garbage removal costs (except by local ordinance) (ORS 90.315; 90.320);

(c) specify that the tenant must bring the rent to the landlord;

(d) require the tenant to notify the landlord of any absence of more than seven days;

(e) impose a late fee;

(f) prohibit subletting or assigning the unit;

(g) prohibit pets;

(h) limit the number of people allowed to occupy the premises;

(i) require the tenant to agree to informal dispute resolution before filing a lawsuit;

(j) impose some kind of "house rules"; and/or

(k) require the tenant to pay a utility or service charge to the landlord when the landlord pays for the service directly for all tenants.

Rules that result in a substantial modification of the bargain cannot be added to the tenant's obligations after a rental agreement is signed unless the tenant consents in writing. (The law is different for mobile home and floating home facilities. See chapter 13.)

Many of these provisions seem advantageous to landlords, although they do have to be in writing to be effective. Unfortunately, many landlords who use written rental agreements use standard forms, some of whose terms are invalid under the law. Landlords who use such forms may expose themselves to liability for attempting to enforce the invalid provisions.

3.2 The advantages of written agreements

Written rental agreements do have some advantages. A written agreement outlining all the rights and responsibilities of the parties not only informs both parties of their obligations, but may also prevent confrontations resulting from poor memories or hasty assessments. Because most proposed contracts are drafted by landlords' interest groups, however, some landlords do not even know what their obligations are until it is too late. (For examples of fair rental agreements, landlords and tenants can contact some of the organizations mentioned in chapter 15.)

A tenant who signs a written agreement is entitled to a copy. If the copy is lost, or if the tenant suspects that his or her copy is different from the landlord's, the tenant has the right to inspect the landlord's copy on reasonable notice and to get a copy, for which the landlord can charge no more than 25 cents per page (ORS 90.305).

In only three circumstances does the law require a written rental agreement:

(a) When the rental agreement is a lease, that is, a rental agreement for a fixed term (six months or one year are common terms)

(b) When the agreement is intended to cover a tenancy longer than one year

(c) When the agreement is for a week-to-week tenancy

3.3 Subletting and written agreements

A tenant is free to sublet or assign the premises without the landlord's consent so long as subletting is not prohibited in a written rental agreement.

In a sublease arrangement, the subtenant is liable to the tenant for the rent, whether the subtenant occupies all or part of the premises. The original tenant remains liable to the landlord in the event the subtenant does not pay or damages the premises.

In the case of an assignment, the new tenant simply takes the place of the old and owes the rent directly to the landlord. The former tenant has no further liability in this situation.

As a practical matter, prohibitions against subletting or assignment are almost never part of an oral rental agreement but are often part of written agreements.

4. Week-to-Week Rentals

To be a week-to-week tenancy, a rental arrangement must have all of these characteristics:

(a) Rent is charged weekly and is payable no less often than every seven days

(b) A written rental agreement defines the parties' rights and responsibilities under the Landlord and Tenant Act

(c) No nonrefundable fees or security deposits are charged (but the landlord may charge an applicant-screening fee) (ORS 90.100).

If the tenancy meets all of these requirements and there is no contrary provision in the rental agreement, the landlord may use shorter notice periods than in month-to-month or term tenancies. In week-to-week tenancies:

(a) The landlord may terminate "for cause" after seven days' written notice with four days to cure. If there is a repeated breach within six months of a termination notice, the landlord may terminate without an opportunity to cure on four days' written notice.

(b) The landlord may raise rent after seven days' notice.

(c) The landlord may serve a 72-hour notice terminating for nonpayment of rent when the tenant fails to pay rent within four days after the day the rent is due.

(d) The time period for no-cause termination notices for week-to-week tenancies is ten days' written notice by either side.

The week-to-week agreement cannot be used for owners of manufactured housing in a facility (ORS 90.400).

5. Teenage Tenants

Because landlords are unsure they can enforce contracts with minors, Oregon law specifically allows many teenagers to make enforceable contracts to rent dwellings. To qualify, the minor must be emancipated and unmarried, living other than with a parent or legal guardian, and —

(a) 16 or 17 years old; or

(b) if under 16, the parent of a child or children living in the minor's physical custody; or

(c) if under 16, pregnant with a child who is expected to live in the physical custody of the minor.

If the underage tenant qualifies as a minor under these rules, the tenant may enter a binding rental agreement with a landlord, and binding contracts with utility providers and vendors of other "necessities of a residential dwelling unit," without the consent of a parent or guardian, and cannot void or disaffirm the contract based on age or status as a minor. The minor's parents or guardians are not liable under the contract unless they become a party to the contract or rental agreement, or execute a separate guarantee agreement.

A landlord may sue to evict such a minor tenant without the court's requiring the appointment of a "guardian ad litem" (usually required for actions against unemancipated minors) for the minor. The landlord could similarly sue the minor for unpaid rent and other damages, just as if the minor were an adult (ORS 105.168).

6. Communications between Landlords and Tenants

Whether a landlord or a tenant, whether under a written or an oral rental agreement, the parties will need to communicate from time to time — to collect rent, ask for repairs, etc. The law sets out some standard rules to help the parties avoid miscommunication and missed communication. ORLTA divides communication between landlords and tenants into two kinds: "actual notice" and written notice (ORS 90.150, 90.155). Sometimes actual notice is good enough to allow a person to enforce a right later on; sometimes written notice is needed.

If actual notice is all that is required, the notice can be given in any of the following ways:

(a) Verbal notice given personally to the landlord or tenant or left on the telephone answering machine of either of them.

(b) Written notice personally delivered to the landlord or tenant, left at the landlord's rental office, sent by facsimile to the landlord's residence or rental office or to the tenant's dwelling, or attached securely to the main entrance to the dwelling of either of them.

(c) Written notice sent by first-class mail, in which case it is considered served three days after it is mailed.

(d) Any other method reasonably calculated to achieve actual receipt of notice, provided the method is listed in a written rental agreement.

When written notice is required by ORLTA, it can be by personal delivery or first-class mail, as above, or, if a written rental agreement provides for this, first-class mail and attachment to a designated location. If the rental agreement says the landlord can give tenants written notice this way, it must also allow tenants to give the landlord notice this way as well. Under a rental agreement that allows for this, the landlord's mailed written notice must be addressed to the tenant at the rented premises; the other copy must go onto the main entrance to the part of the premises where the tenant lives (as opposed to the main entrance to an entire apartment building, for example), and it must be attached "in a secure manner." The tenant's mailed notice to the landlord under this kind of agreement must go to the landlord at an address designated in the rental agreement. The second copy of the tenant's notice is to be securely attached to a clearly described location designated in the rental agreement. That location must be reasonably located in relation to the tenant and available at all hours.

Like the "actual notice" described above, written notices are deemed to be served three days after they have been mailed by regular first-class mail. Landlords and tenants can use other ways to reach each other in addition to, but not instead of, the methods described above.

CHAPTER FOUR

FEES AND DEPOSITS

Landlords more and more commonly charge a variety of fees and deposits, some of them lawful and some not. Regrettably, wrongfully charged fees and withheld deposits are the most common abuse of tenants' rights by uninformed or dishonest landlords. Astute landlords are careful to avoid liability for misapplying the law in an area that is rapidly becoming more complex. It's also crucial for tenants to know their rights about fees and deposits — after all, it's their money at stake. Unfortunately, tenants rarely take the necessary steps when they move in to protect their rights when they move out.

1. When Can a Landlord Charge Fees and Deposits?

An allowable fee in all kinds of tenancies is an application fee (limited by ORS 90.140; see chapter 2). In month-to-month and fixed-term agreements, landlords can require cleaning fees, late fees, and other fees for specific purposes. Landlords may even charge penalties for noncompliance with a written rental agreement if the agreement allows. With a few exceptions described below, a fee can be charged only one time during a tenancy (ORS 90.302). Deposits can include hold deposits, cleaning deposits, security deposits, key deposits, and prepaid rent ("last month's rent") deposits.

Landlords should make it a regular business practice to provide receipts for fees, deposits, and rent payments. Tenants who ask in writing for receipts for deposits and rent payments (at the time they offer the payment) don't have to make the payment if the landlord fails to provide the receipts. Landlords must provide receipts for fees whether the tenant asks for them or not (ORS 90.302). The receipt needs to show only the amount paid, the date of payment, and information identifying the landlord (ORS 90.140). It does not have to be on a special form. For payments made by mail or bank transfer, when the landlord is not present for the delivery of the payment, the landlord is obliged to provide a receipt promptly (ORS 90.150 (2)–(3)).

1.1 Is it a deposit or a fee?

There are two basic differences between fees and deposits. Fees are not refundable. All deposits are refundable unless the tenant does something to entitle the landlord to keep the money. For example, the landlord can keep the deposit if he or she offers a unit to the applicant and the applicant gives the landlord a deposit to hold the unit, but then the tenant doesn't take it. Another example would be if a tenant gives the landlord a cleaning deposit, then he or she moves out leaving a mess that forces the landlord to use the entire deposit to clean the place.

Another difference between fees and deposits is that fees can be charged only for a specific, reasonably anticipated landlord expense and the fees cannot be excessive. There is no limit, in contrast, on the amount of deposit a landlord can require at the beginning of a tenancy.

1.2 Deposits

Deposits — money belonging to the tenant and held by the landlord as a kind of insurance if the tenant doesn't do what is promised — are the most typical kinds of payments landlords ask for at the beginning of a tenancy. An amount simply labeled "deposit" or "security deposit" can be used for many purposes: to cover any losses caused by the tenant's failure to live up to the rental agreement and for any expenses for repairs at the end of the tenancy beyond normal wear and tear (beyond what might be covered by a specific fee), so long as the tenant caused repairs to be needed.

A "last month's rent" deposit serves the more limited purpose of making sure that the landlord gets the rent for the last month the tenant is in the unit; it cannot be used to pay for repairs when the tenant moves out or for any other purpose. Also, in some situations, a landlord cannot serve an eviction notice and ask a court to evict a tenant "before the expiration of any period for which the tenant … has paid the rent … in advance." Exceptions to this rule are discussed in chapter 8.

Likewise, a deposit labeled "cleaning deposit" may be used only for that purpose and not for any unpaid rent or other purposes.

A "key deposit" provides tenants with an incentive not to move away without returning their dwelling keys to the landlord, thereby forcing a conscientious landlord to re-key the unit to protect the security of the next tenants. A key "fee," on the other hand, is unlawful because the tenant is entitled to get into the place he or she is renting.

Landlords cannot lawfully demand a "security deposit" from tenants with disabilities who are allowed to make reasonable modifications to their units at their own expense. In fact, public housing agencies cannot require tenants to pay for these modifications. If the unit would be unusable by others who move in after such a tenant moves out, landlords in these cases can require the tenant to open an escrow account to cover the cost of changing the unit back when the tenant leaves (see chapter 14).

During the first year of a tenancy, the landlord may not require any additional security deposits from the tenant, unless the parties agree to change the terms and conditions of the rental agreement to permit a pet or for another reason and use the increased deposit for that purpose. A landlord can insist on an additional deposit after the first year, but in that case the tenant has three months in which to pay the increase. Landlords must be careful not to base a new deposit amount on an increase in the number of children in a household, as a court would likely view the increase as discriminatory (see chapter 14).

It is helpful to tenants and landlords (and judges) for landlords to label the payments clearly on a receipt. A deposit for property damage should be labeled as such; a "damage deposit" may get confused with the broader legal concept of "damages," which means anything for which a court might award a judgment for money. The same principles apply to fees. Try to make the purpose of the payment as clear and as specific as possible to reduce arguments at the end of the tenancy about whether or which money needs to be returned.

Oregon law does not require landlords to give tenants interest on their deposits. Unless the landlord and tenant agree otherwise, professional property managers must allow the interest on the deposits they hold to go to the Oregon Housing and Community Services Department to fund low-income housing. A tenant can certainly negotiate with the landlord at the inception of the tenancy to receive the interest, or a portion of the interest, at the end of the tenancy.

New landlords should take note that they are responsible for the security deposits paid to their predecessor landlord, even if that landlord has pocketed the money (ORS 90.302).

1.3 Application fees

Application fees are lawful for all kinds of tenancies in Oregon, subject to some restrictions (see chapter 2).

In month-to-month and fixed-term agreements only, landlords can require cleaning fees, late fees, and other fees for the specific purposes described below.

1.4 Late fees

A landlord may not charge a late fee under an oral rental agreement or in a week-to-week rental. Furthermore, under ORS 90.260, a landlord may not impose a late payment charge even with a written rental agreement unless —

(a) the rent is not received by the end of the fourth day of the weekly or monthly rental period for which rent is payable,

(b) the rental agreement provides for late charges and states the rental due date and the date on which a late charge becomes payable, and

(c) the rental agreement describes the type and amount of the late charge. (When a landlord offers a "discount" for early payment, the difference between the "discount" price and the "regular" rent is a late fee, which cannot be imposed until the fifth day of the regular rental period.)

The statute has two other simple provisions: first, that nonpayment of a late fee alone shall not constitute grounds for eviction for nonpayment of rent; second, that a landlord may not deduct late charges from future rent payments, thereby making that rent payment delinquent. Note that late payments can be the basis of a 30-day eviction notice without cause for month-to-month tenants or the basis of an eviction notice for cause (depending on the terms of the rental agreement).

How much can a landlord charge as a late fee? The landlord can choose from three options:

(a) A reasonable flat fee, charged once per rental period (with "reasonable" meaning whatever amount is customarily charged in that rental market).

(b) A reasonable amount charged on a per-day basis, starting on the fifth day of the rental period for which rent is overdue. The daily charge may accrue throughout the rental period until the rent — not including the late charge — is paid in full. At the end of the rental period, the daily charge must stop. The total amount of the charge cannot exceed 6 percent of an amount that would constitute a reasonable flat fee amount described in (a), above.

(c) An amount equal to 5 percent of the rent, charged for each five-day period, or portion of a five-day period, for which the rent is overdue, beginning on the fifth day of the rental period and accumulating until that rent payment — not including the late charge — is paid in full. At the end of the rent period, the late fee stops accruing.

A landlord can charge interest on unpaid late charges at the rate allowed for judgments — currently a hefty 9 percent. The interest will continue to accrue even after the late charge itself stops.

1.5 Dishonored check fees and miscellaneous fees and charges

ORS 90.302 authorizes landlords to incorporate in written rental agreements a charge for returned checks; they also can list a charge against tenants for tampering with a properly working smoke alarm or detector or for other violations of the written rental agreement that specify a penalty fee.

As technology has become more a part of everyday living — specifically cable and satellite TV, video subscription service, Internet access and use — some landlords have contracted with providers of these services for discounted access for all the tenants in a complex. (Usually landlords do this because the provider refuses to contract with individual tenants.) Under ORS 90.315, it is lawful for landlords who have done this to charge all new tenants for the service regardless of whether they will use it, provided that —

(a) a written rental agreement provides for the charge;

(b) the charge for the service, if it includes a surcharge that goes to the landlord as profit, is no more than 10 per cent over the charge the tenant must pay and is less altogether than the amount the tenant would have to pay at retail prices; and

(c) existing tenants are not charged for the service if it is not included in their original rental agreement.

A violation of any of these provisions can result in damages to the tenant of the larger of one month's rent or twice the amount wrongfully charged.

Sometimes a prospective tenant who wants these services will prepare to move into a complex only to learn that either the previous tenant did not pay the charges or that the landlord has not paid the provider, so the promised service doesn't exist. In that case, the prospective tenant can —

(a) immediately terminate the rental agreement by giving the landlord actual notice and the reason for the termination, or

(b) pay the outstanding amount and deduct it from the rent, or

(c) enter into an agreement with the landlord to resolve the problem. (Obviously, if the landlord is the one who hasn't been paying, this exercise will likely be a waste of the tenant's time.)

If the prospective tenant chooses to terminate the tenancy, the landlord must return all deposits, rents, and fees within four days.

If the tenant does not find out about the problem until he or she has already moved in, the choices are slightly different. The tenant can —

(a) pay the amount and deduct it from the rent, or

(b) terminate the rental agreement by giving the landlord 72 hours' actual notice but also giving the landlord that much time to fix the problem and keep the tenant from terminating.

If the tenant decides to terminate, his or her damages depend on who the rental agreement says is responsible for obtaining the service. If the tenant is responsible, the tenant's damages are "actual damages" — the tenant's out-of-pocket costs caused by the lack of the service — plus all rent, fees, and deposits. The actual damages will vary depending on the tenant's individual situation. They may even include move-in and move-out costs. If the landlord is responsible and either does not provide the service or allows it to be cut off for nonpayment, the tenant's damages are all rent prepaid for the month of the termination prorated to the date the tenant leaves, all other prepaid rent, and all of the security deposit. In both situations the landlord must return this money within four days. If the landlord does not return the money in a timely manner, the tenant is entitled to twice the amount wrongfully withheld.

In the event a tenant decides not to pay a valid charge for utilities or services, the landlord cannot use the failure to pay as grounds for a nonpayment-of-rent eviction (requiring only 72 hours' notice with an opportunity to cure). However, the landlord can terminate the tenancy "for cause" using a 30-day notice (see chapter 8).

2. How Landlords Can Minimize Damage to Rental Units

Conscientious landlords are exasperated by tenants who don't mention the need for repairs until move-out day, when a problem may have become much more expensive to fix than if the tenant had alerted the landlord earlier. These landlords need to remember that many tenants have been "trained" by unscrupulous landlords that to report a problem elicits a no-cause eviction notice in response. Other tenants simply don't realize they have a duty to report. By encouraging tenants to report problems and by making prompt repairs, landlords can gain the tenants' trust and avert many such problems.

Landlords can help tenants minimize accidental harm to their rentals by explaining things that might be new to particular tenants. For example, if a tenant has never used a dishwasher or has used only dishwashers with built-in disposals, the tenant may not know that the dishwasher you have supplied will malfunction if dishes aren't rinsed and scraped before going into the machine. There is also many a tenant — and homeowner — who has unintentionally destroyed an ancient freezer by trying to defrost it with a knife. Likewise, tenants don't necessarily know that drain cleaners that work well with septic systems work poorly with sewage lines. Other things tenants may not be aware of is that some kitchen counters are sensitive to hot pans; some are not, some linoleum floors accept waxing; some don't, and a cleanser that works effectively on porcelain may scratch "marble" sinks and fixtures. Tenants will welcome information about how best to maintain their home.

3. How Tenants Can Protect Their Security Deposits and Prevent Getting Sued for Damage

One of the most common complaints tenants have is that their former landlord "stole" their security deposit. Unfortunately, that word is sometimes accurate. Some unscrupulous landlords even sue their former tenants for damage to the unit the tenant did not cause.

There are things tenants can do to protect their deposits and make sure they are not held responsible for damage they didn't do. The time to take precautions is at the beginning — not the end — of the tenancy. First, tenants should be sure to ask in writing for receipts for all deposits, keeping a copy of the dated request. They should attempt to label the deposit carefully. Tenants need to keep the copy of the request and the receipt until their tenancy is over and they have their money in hand again.

The second thing they need to do — and just as important — is to document the condition of the rental at the time of move-in.

3.1 The move-in inspection

As a practical matter, a tenant who has spent the last two or three days cleaning the last home and packing and moving belongings isn't going to have much enthusiasm to start a new tenancy with a major inspection. It's important to remember that a thoroughly documented move-in inspection can be worth hundreds of dollars later.

How should you go about assessing conditions? The most aggressive approach possible when protecting yourself against unwarranted damage claims is to demand an inspection from your local building agency and have the inspector attach the report to the rental agreement, along with the landlord's promise to repair all defects. However, many communities don't provide such a service, and in any event, the inspection won't cover many of the things that a landlord might charge you for later (e.g., a chip in the porcelain in the bathtub or a large stain in a carpet).

It is more common to go through the premises with the landlord, before signing or paying for anything, and make an exhaustive list of all the defects you can find. Note every condition of dirt, wear, and damage and any deterioration of every floor, wall, door, ceiling, fixture, and window. Don't forget to see if everything works; for example, lights, drains, hot water, and heat. Also, inspect every item of furniture and appliance furnished by the landlord. When you think you're through, the safest proof of the state in which you found the premises is to have the inventory of what you found signed by both you and the landlord.

Also helpful are detailed photographs or video footage showing such seemingly insignificant flaws as pinholes in walls, scratches in windows and linoleum, and scrapes or nicks in tubs, sinks, and refrigerator. (Be sure to photograph the insides of sinks, toilets, refrigerator, and stove.) Date the backs of the photos. Having a reliable witness (someone who will likely still be around when you move out) walk through the place and take notes can also be invaluable.

If the ownership of the property changes during your tenancy, witness statements and photos or videotapes of the condition at move-in can be especially important. The new landlord will not know how the place looked before the purchase. You should be aware that new owners are liable for the return of deposits made to their predecessors; this news comes as a surprise to many fledgling owners.

Remember that you are trying to protect yourself against damage claims as well as uncover needed repairs. Your findings will have an important bearing on any later dispute regarding the extent of normal wear and tear.

"Normal wear and tear" is the deterioration of a dwelling that is to be expected from reasonable use as a dwelling over time; things wear out. Unfortunately, some landlords do not understand that a tenant should not be liable for the cost of replacing a completely worn out stove or carpet or bathroom floor, even though those things are the natural result of normal wear and tear. Normal wear and tear does not include the results of negligent or deliberate misuse.

You may not have time before moving in to make an exhaustive inspection, or you may have good reason not to press the landlord for a jointly signed statement. Another approach, once you've made your inspection, is to write a letter to the landlord that includes your list of defects (see Sample 2). The longer you wait to do this, the more likely it is that the landlord may claim that you caused the problems.

SAMPLE 2
LETTER TO LANDLORD DESCRIBING DEFECTS

November 5, 20--

Dear Ms. Smith:

After I moved into the house I rented from you on November 1, 20--, I took the time to make a careful inspection. So that you know I am not to blame for damage and wear that I noticed, I am enclosing a list that describes everything I found. If you want to confirm these things for yourself, please call me at 555-555-5555 to arrange for an inspection. I can usually be reached after 5:30 p.m.

Sincerely,

I.M. Tenant

I.M. Tenant

enclosure: list of defects

3.1a   Get a witness for your inspection of the place

Particularly if your landlord declines to verify your list of defects, it is a good idea to get a friend to witness it. Try to get someone a judge is likely to believe and who will be around when you move out. Have him or her inspect your place as soon as possible after you move in and sign a statement like the one in Sample 3 at the end of your list.

3.1b   Discovering repairs needed

If you find serious problems you want fixed, it is important that you point them out as soon as possible. Although a landlord should not be able to claim that you waived the right to have him

SAMPLE 3
STATEMENT OF WITNESS REGARDING
CONDITION OF PREMISES

On November 6, 20--, I personally inspected the home of I.M. Witness (tenant name), at 123 Tenant Avenue (tenant address), and verified the existence of every condition listed above.

Wally Witness,
November 6, 20--

Wally Witness
(Witness signature, with date)

SAMPLE 4
PARAGRAPH DEMANDING REPAIRS

I placed a check mark next to some of the items on this list that I believe violate the Landlord and Tenant Act. Please call me at 555-555-5555 to arrange access to the house or to discuss the best way to fix the problems as soon as possible.

or her make repairs required by ORLTA, your not saying anything about them may provide a strong argument that they really didn't bother you much at the time and therefore aren't worth much by way of damages or as a set-off against the rent.

To demand repairs, add a paragraph similar to the one in Sample 4 to your inspection letter. (Note: Always keep a copy of everything and be sure you date your documents.)

Of course, asking for repairs involves some risk. If you're in doubt, send a letter similar to Sample 2 right away, then read chapters 5 and 6. If you want to demand repairs, send a letter of the sort described in chapter 5. Remember that by making a written demand for repairs without stating the times convenient for you to have them made, you are giving the landlord the right to enter at any objectively reasonable time over the next seven days (see chapter 1).

You will be glad you went through all this trouble when the landlord claims that he or she has to refinish the hardwood floors because of you when it was the former tenant who had the 19 cats!

3.1c Documenting ownership of appliances and furniture

Although they are less common, disputes occasionally arise over the ownership of appliances and furniture. Sometimes a tenant moves out a stove at the end of a tenancy only to find that the landlord claims it was provided by and belongs to the landlord. The procedure outlined above can be modified to protect you against such a dispute.

If items of furniture and appliances are not listed in a rental agreement, you can send a list to the landlord with a letter inviting corrections or additions; or get a credible witness to sign your list; or both. Of course, if the landlord responds and disagrees, make sure you reply with any corrections promptly. Understand that a dishonest former tenant may have removed something that belongs to the landlord or replaced an appliance with a cheaper one. Be sure your list specifies the brand and model of all appliances furnished by the landlord so you don't discover a former tenant's swap for the first time when your landlord accuses you of replacing an electric range with a wood burner when you move out.

3.2 Getting back a deposit at the end of a tenancy

ORLTA entitles a tenant to the return of any unused portion of a deposit unless the deposit was paid to hold the unit until the signing of the rental agreement (in which case it should have been credited as part of the first month's rent), or unless the payment was a fee. A landlord who wrongfully withholds any portion of a deposit, or any prepaid rent, for more than 31 days after termination of the tenancy and delivery of possession, or who fails to account in writing to the tenant within that period for any deductions, is liable to the tenant for twice the amount wrongfully withheld or withheld in bad faith (ORS 90.302). (In limited circumstances, a landlord has a duty to return deposits and prepaid rent significantly sooner. See chapter 10.) In addition, a landlord who has charged a fee and a deposit for the same purpose must apply the fee to any expense first, and the deposit to any cost remaining.

Some landlords are eager to walk through a unit with a tenant at the end of the tenancy to inspect and, if the tenant is lucky, return either all or a portion of the deposit at that time. Conscientious landlords try to do a walk-through before the tenant moves out so that they know precisely what the condition of the unit is before they let someone else move in. This is not required by law — unfortunately for tenants who could use both the money and the peace of mind — and many landlords do not in fact conduct a move-out walk-through with tenants. If your landlord accepts an invitation to inspect with you at move-out time, it is useful to have a witness present to hear the landlord's assessment of the condition of the place.

You should let your landlord know where to send your money by leaving a forwarding address, preferably by sending a letter (as always, keep a copy). If you can itemize what is due, do so. If you think there is a reasonable claim for damages beyond normal wear and tear, it is usually safest to get the problem fixed yourself at minimal expense before you leave, rather than giving the landlord a chance to spend your money on the repair without concern about a fair cost. Sample 5 is an example of the kind of letter you could send. (Of course, if you think you're entitled to all of your deposit back, your letter should say so.)

If you have good reason to believe that your landlord is in the habit of ripping off tenants for deposits, you can deduct the portion of the deposit you feel you are entitled to from your last rent payment. Let your landlord know you are doing so by sending a letter similar to the one in Sample 6. The worst that can lawfully happen is that the landlord will serve you with a 72-hour notice for not paying the rent. After receiving the notice, you will have 72 hours to decide whether to pay the difference, contest the eviction, or move out before the eviction judgment can be enforced against you (see chapter 8). A judgment against you can result in your being "blacklisted." (See chapter 2, section 2.2.)

In any event, if the landlord hasn't returned the money you think you're entitled to on the day you move out, you will need to document the condition of the unit. Again, take detailed photographs or video footage and get a friend to come look at your place just before you move out in case you need a witness. This can be the same person who saw the premises when you moved in.

SAMPLE 5
LETTER DEMANDING RETURN OF PART
OF THE DEPOSIT

August 30, 20--

Dear Mr. Smith:

As I notified you earlier, today I am terminating my tenancy at 123 Tenant Lane, Portland, Oregon. As you will recall, I paid a last month's rent of $500, a key deposit of $10, a cleaning deposit of $250, and a damage deposit of $300 when I moved in.

By my calculations, I am entitled to the return of one-third of the prepaid rent, or $166. Since I am returning the keys with this letter, I am also entitled to the $10 key deposit. As you will see, I am leaving the place cleaner than it was when I moved in, so I am entitled to get back the entire $250 cleaning deposit. I fixed the screen door you were worried about, and there is one broken window pane in the bathroom that I am responsible for. Ace Hardware gave me an estimate of $35 to fix it, so I would like $265 of the damage deposit back.

Please send a check for the total amount, $691, to me at 444 Happy Street, Coos Bay, Oregon, 98888.

Sincerely,

I.M. Tenant

I.M. Tenant

Enclosure: 2 keys

SAMPLE 6
LETTER TO LANDLORD EXPLAINING DEDUCTION OF
DEPOSIT FROM RENT

August 15, 20--

Dear Mr. Smith:

As I advised you earlier, my tenancy at 123 Tenant Lane, Portland, Oregon, will end on August 30, 20--. As you recall, I paid a deposit of $350 when I moved in. I am deducting the portion of the deposit to which I think I am entitled from the rent payment that is enclosed in this letter. I am doing this because it will save you the trouble of figuring out how much to return, the place is cleaner than it was when I moved in, the screen door you complained about last month has been repaired, and Ace Hardware will be replacing the bathroom window glass for $30.

As my rent is $600, I am enclosing $280. If you accept this money as payment in full, I hereby release you from your obligation to return the deposit. You are welcome to inspect the place to see if you need to claim any more for the deposit, by coming between 5 p.m. and 6 p.m. of any weekday next week.

Sincerely,

I.M. Tenant

I.M. Tenant

enclosure: rent check

3.3 Why landlords withhold deposits

Most landlords who withhold deposits do so legitimately, but some make up or exaggerate damage claims after their tenants move out. This practice has led many states to adopt special statutes governing deposits.

In Oregon, a landlord must submit to the tenant an accounting in writing for all deductions claimed and must do so within 31 days of the termination of the tenancy. The landlord must make a separate accounting for deposits and for prepaid rent. If any portion is wrongfully withheld, the tenant is entitled to recover twice that amount. Any amount withheld without an accounting is wrongfully withheld under the statute, as is any amount withheld in bad faith, including amounts withheld on the basis of dishonest accounting.

A security deposit is refundable unless the landlord has had to use all or part of it to cover the reasonable expenses of curing a problem — beyond normal wear and tear — caused by the tenant. The problem must be one related to the purposes for which the deposit was paid. Unless the parties have specified a more limited purpose for the deposit at the beginning of the tenancy, a security deposit can be used for the following purposes only:

(a) To make up for tenant's failure to abide by his or her side of the rental agreement; for example, the duty to pay the rent

(b) To repair damage to the premises caused by the tenant, not including ordinary wear and tear

A security deposit may not be used as a penalty for the tenant's failure to stay for a specified term, although a fee may be charged for this purpose. Any portion of the deposit that is not used for the purposes listed above must be returned to the tenant. The landlord has a duty to mitigate damages, which means that he or she cannot choose an unnecessarily expensive way in which to cure any problems caused by the tenant. Furthermore, a landlord who charges both a fee and a deposit for the same purpose must deduct costs first from the fee.

While a last month's rent deposit is supposed to secure the payment of the rent for the last month of the tenancy, "prepaid rent" is money paid to the landlord before the payment is due. It also means rent paid for a period beyond the termination date. A landlord should generally return prepaid rent to the tenant if this payment covers a period of time after the tenant leaves and after the termination of the tenancy.

For example, a tenant who terminates a tenancy by serving a "fix it or I'm leaving" notice (see chapter 10) is entitled to the return of all unused security and prepaid rent. The same is true of a tenant who terminates because of a landlord's retaliation, lockout, or utility shutoff. A tenant who terminates because of a landlord's abuse of the right of access is entitled to the return of unused security deposits and is also entitled to recover at least one month's rent as damages. Finally, a tenant who exercises the right to terminate because of a serious and imminent threat to the health or safety of occupants not caused by the tenant (see chapter 10) is entitled to a return of all security deposits (including any last month's rent) and all rent prepaid for the month in which the termination occurs if the condition existed at the outset of the tenancy.

A tenant who leaves before the expiration of the tenants' 30-day notice to the landlord is not entitled to a refund of the rent covering the rest of the 30 days unless the parties have agreed otherwise, a new tenant moves in before the 30 days expire, or the tenant is exercising some special right to terminate the tenancy on an earlier date.

Because a landlord may end a month-to-month tenancy by serving a 30-day notice to terminate the tenancy on any day during the rent period, it is possible for the termination date to occur before the end of a period for which the tenant has paid rent. The landlord cannot start an eviction case based on nonpayment of rent before any prepaid rent is used up; if the tenant moves out voluntarily, however, rent is apportioned day to day, and the tenant is entitled to a refund of any balance. A landlord can terminate a week-to-week tenancy only at the end of a rent period, so the problem of unused regular rent should not arise in this kind of tenancy. Prepaid rent for later weeks still would be due to the tenant, who may even have the right to stay if the termination notice was based on "no cause." See Chapter 8.

The purpose of any last month's rent payment (or any similar deposit) is to protect the landlord against a tenant's failure to make the last rent payment. For this reason, it fits the definition of "security deposit," and any portion not used for that purpose must be returned to the tenant.

3.4 Small claims court

If all else fails, a tenant may face taking the former landlord to small claims court to get back a deposit. A landlord, likewise, may be seeking damages for harm to the rental beyond what the landlord obtained in deposits or fees. If represented by a lawyer, the person could file the claim in a regular court, but this may not be practical. It may be hard to find an attorney willing to take the case when there is little money at stake, because a court is unlikely to award a substantial fee. Small claims court, on the other hand, is designed for people to represent themselves. It is also relatively speedy and informal. In some counties, the court offers a mediation service as part of the small claims process. This may be the most comfortable way to resolve the dispute.

You cannot seek more than $5,000 in small claims court. If you ask for more than $750, your opponent has the option of making you start over in regular court, filing new papers, and paying new fees. In counties without court mediation programs that cover small claims or landlord-tenant disputes, moving the case into regular court will require submitting your case to an arbitrator first. The purpose of arbitration is to resolve issues outside the courtroom, saving parties (and the court) time and money. Unfortunately, the cost of arbitration is often as high as the claim at stake. Instead of encouraging settlements, it has had the effect of discouraging people from filing claims at all.

If your opponent responds to your small claims complaint by filing a claim against you in your case (i.e., by "counterclaiming"), the case will be transferred to regular court if that counterclaim exceeds the small claims limit. Arbitration will again be part of the process. If the case goes to trial, either side may request a jury (a change that complicates the case greatly and costs even more money).

If the case stays in small claims court and you lose, whether you have the right to appeal will depend on where you live.

If your case was heard where small claims court is a division of the regular court, there is no appeal. If it was heard in justice court, on the other hand, things get a bit more complicated. Neither side can appeal a judgment for less than $30. Neither side can appeal a judgment denying a claim filed by that side. On the other hand, both sides may appeal a judgment for $30 or more rendered against the side that wants to appeal.

In other words, if you file a claim against your landlord and you win, your landlord can appeal. If you lose, you can't appeal. If the landlord files a counterclaim against you and you lose on that counterclaim, you can appeal that loss. If the landlord loses on that counterclaim, the landlord cannot appeal that loss. If you have the right to appeal, the time limit is short — only ten days.

Before you file your case, assess whether your landlord will file a counterclaim against you (for damage, unpaid rent, etc.) that the landlord is likely to win. Filing in that situation would be a mistake. Assuming that you are confident about your case, however, you must make some attempt to collect the amount you claim before going to court. A letter like the one in Sample 5 demanding that the landlord return your money is all that is necessary. The clerk of the small claims court will ask you to sign an affidavit saying that you tried to collect your money before filing your claim. The judge may want to see a copy of your letter when the case is heard, so be sure to keep a copy.

One more thing tenants should do before actually filing their claim is to decide whom to sue. The person you assume is the owner may only be an agent or manager. You should have been given a written statement about this at the beginning of the tenancy and at any time after that if the information changed. You can find out the name of the owner by asking at the county tax office.

If you were not given a written statement and if you find the owner was not the person you suspected, you can have the real landlord "served" (given formal notice of the small claims action) by directing the sheriff to hand the summons and complaint to any nondisclosing manager as agent of the landlord for service of process. Also, such a person can be required to perform the landlord's obligations — including returning deposits — so you can sue him or her as well as the real landlord. If you are going to try to use these rights, make sure you take a copy of ORLTA with you every time you go to court; you may have to use it to explain to the clerk or the judge what you're doing.

If you have trouble finding a defendant to sue, remember that a lot of people may fit the definition of "landlord" under the law. Also note that anyone who holds the landlord's interest in the property at the time of the termination of the tenancy is liable for unreturned deposits.

When you learn your hearing date, ask the court clerk to assist you with subpoenas if you need them. On court day, have your evidence and witnesses on hand. Your evidence could include:

(a) Receipts for everything you paid to the landlord (it's best to bring your rent receipts for the entire tenancy)

(b) A list, photograph, or other similar evidence of what the place was like when you moved in

(c) A copy of any letters you sent to the landlord about the deposit

(d) Witnesses to the condition of the place when you moved in and when you moved out

Also take a copy of ORLTA. Prepare a short outline of what you have to say. Be brief and to the point.

Your witnesses should be people who personally observed the condition of the premises. A witness who has to rely on the observations of other people isn't worth much unless he or she heard your opponent say something damaging to your opponent's case. Point out that if the landlord failed to account in writing for any deductions within 31 days after the end of the tenancy, the landlord cannot claim a deduction. On the other hand, if the landlord is entitled to keep some of the deposit, say so.

Landlords can expect to have to provide evidence of their claims or counterclaims for damages, typically using the same kinds of evidence — photographs or similar evidence of the premises before the tenant moved in and after the tenant moved out, receipts for costs of cleaning and repair, etc.

When deciding whether to go to court, remember that the landlord has a right to counterclaim for damages to the premises or for rent due. If you owe rent or damaged the premises, it might be best to leave well enough alone, even if there was no accounting. Remember also that you have one year from the date the landlord should have returned your money and/or given you an accounting in which to file your lawsuit. After that, it is too late.

CHAPTER FIVE

"IF YOU DON'T LIKE IT, WHY DON'T YOU MOVE?"

ORLTA is based on the idea that responsible tenants will report habitability problems promptly to their landlords, and that their landlords, relieved to hear about the problem before it gets worse and more expensive, provide prompt, competent repairs. This chapter and chapter 6 describe the options for responsible tenants who have irresponsible landlords — the kind who say, "If you don't like it, why don't you move?" or say nothing and then present the tenant with an eviction notice. These two chapters are for tenants who want to stay in their homes and enforce their rights. (Tenants who are fed up and ready to leave if the landlord won't cooperate and tenants who have to leave because the problems are so severe should go straight to chapter 10.)

ORLTA tries to motivate landlords like these to conform to the law by offering damages to wronged tenants and, in some cases, injunctive relief. ("Damages" refer to the amount of money the tenant is awarded.) ORLTA puts damages for wronged tenants in three general categories:

- *General or actual damages:* This means the kinds of harm that flow naturally from the kind of wrong done, such as a reduction in the value of the rental unit caused by habitability problems.

- *Special damages:* This term refers to out-of-pocket costs to fix problems the landlord refuses to fix, or medical bills caused by a problem at the rental such as impure water.

- *Statutory damages:* This term means money in a specific amount to compensate for specific harms, like twice the amount of a security deposit wrongfully withheld by a landlord.

In extreme cases, tenants have even been awarded damages for the emotional distress their landlord caused them when they tried to enforce their rights. In housing discrimination cases, wronged tenants are generally awarded damages for the indignity to which the landlord subjected them. "Injunctive relief" (also known as an injunction or a restraining order) is an order from the court forcing someone to do something or be held in contempt of court (for example, forcing a landlord to stop violating ORLTA by replacing a badly deteriorated roof).

As you read these chapters, bear in mind that each remedy (except suing the landlord) has two functions: to get repairs without ending up in court, and to equip you with proof to defend against an eviction if you do end up in court. All of these remedies can be used by tenants acting together in a tenants' union; concerted action can be the most effective remedy of all (see chapter 15).

1. Reporting a Habitability Problem

Tenants do not have to report most kinds of habitability violations in writing, but they have a duty to notify their landlord of habitability problems as soon as they arise. (It is necessary to report in writing malfunctioning smoke alarms and "repair and deduct" notices for appliances and essential services — see chapter 6.) However, putting requests in writing is an excellent idea. Putting them in writing politely is an even better idea, but the most crucial thing to remember is to keep all copies of correspondence.

When you have done this and the landlord doesn't do anything about the problem within a reasonable amount of time, you will need to make some decisions about what to do next. Ideally, all tenants should have the assistance of an attorney well versed in landlord and tenant law before making this kind of decision. Small factual variations in your situation may critically affect your rights or chances of success, and courts or the legislature may have changed the law since this book was written.

As a practical matter, however, few tenants with repair problems can afford this kind of consultation. You may have to do everything yourself, with the knowledge that an attempt at eviction is often the reaction tenants get when they assert their rights.

2. Demand Letters

If your first, informal request for repairs didn't work, your next step is usually a demand letter or a building inspection (see section 3. below).

A demand letter is simply a written request, usually mailed, preferably by both regular and certified mail, stating your request for repairs. (Sample 7 shows a simple demand for repairs.) It has two functions:

(a) To make your position known to the landlord in precise terms.

(b) To prove that you have done so. Keep copies of everything, and make sure your letters are dated.

2.1 Why use a demand letter?

Even if you use one of the rent-withholding remedies (described in chapter 6) that do not require prior written notice, the judge or jury will definitely want to know whether the landlord actually knew of your complaints. Moreover, a dated demand letter will help you prove that your complaints to a landlord came before an eviction notice in case you want to prove the landlord is retaliating against you for asserting your rights (see chapter 8).

2.1a Special Damages

A demand letter may also be important to a tenant's right to recover special damages either as a judgment for money from the landlord or as a court's reduction in the amount of rent owed. Such things as damage to personal possessions caused by a water leak, or theft caused by faulty locks, amount to special damages because they depend on the additional effects caused by the particular problem.

It is not necessary to prove that the landlord knew of any risks of special damages before you can recover money (or reduce the landlord's claim for rent) because of those damages. On the other hand, the law assumes a reduction in rental value flows from any substantial failure of the landlord to supply housing that meets the habitability standards of the law, and you will not have to prove the landlord knew such general damages would result from the violations. (You do, of course, have to prove the violations occurred.)

2.1b Emotional Distress

A demand letter may also help you recover damages for "emotional distress" (also called "mental suffering" or "mental anguish") if you have suffered substantial anxiety as a result of your landlord's violations of the law and if these violations are deliberate misconduct such as lockouts, utility shutoffs, and retaliation. Tenants who suffer severe emotional distress because of a landlord's conduct that is "outrageous in the extreme" may recover emotional distress damages under the common law rather than under ORLTA or other statutes.

If your situation involves a substantial risk of emotional distress, identify that risk in your demand letter in the hope that your letter will prevent the harm you fear. If it doesn't, it may help you recover damages (or reduce any rent owed) resulting from that harm by proving the landlord knew of the risk.

2.2 Negotiating and compromising

If you do get a response to your demand letter, the next step is to negotiate an acceptable solution to the dispute and to get a settlement in writing. Make sure you cover everything so that the landlord can't argue that you waived a complaint. Both parties should keep a signed copy of the agreement, as well as copies of any receipts. Even if the landlord won't sign an agreement, you can send a letter to the landlord outlining your understanding of the oral agreement and asking the landlord to contact you if your understanding is incorrect.

You may want to suggest solutions that will save the landlord some work without reducing your rights. For example, you might offer to arrange for the plumber and pay for the work out of the next rent check. This way, you may have more control over the timing and over the quality of the work than if you were to force the landlord to find the labor. If you and the landlord agree to do this, don't agree to an expense limit with the landlord without first obtaining a binding estimate. However, many landlords have maintenance people they use regularly — although many of these people don't have the skill needed to do the job competently.

SAMPLE 7
LETTER DEMANDING REPAIRS
(BEFORE BUILDING INSPECTION)

November 15, 20--

Dear Ms. Smith:

Over the past two weeks, I have asked you 10 times to do something about the fact that we have no heat and our front door won't lock. Although I have made every attempt to allow you to investigate these problems, you have not made any of the repairs requested. I will be forced to call for a building inspection if you do not make repairs voluntarily.

If I do not hear from you by November 22, 20--, I will have the apartment inspected and will seek legal assistance to enforce my rights. I look forward to your prompt cooperation.

Sincerely,

I.M. Tenant

I.M. Tenant

One way to encourage the landlord to do the work quickly is to agree that part of the rent will be withheld until the work has been completed. This is an arrangement the landlord may or may not be willing to accept. Remember that a tenant is entitled to damages for, and even a court order for repairs of, substantial violations of the habitability provisions of the law.

It is often effective to provide the landlord with copies of the relevant provisions of the law as you discuss the problem. Once you convince your landlord that he or she may be liable for damages for past violations, you might offer to release him or her from the liability if he or she promptly complies with a request that isn't required by the act (e.g., providing paint).

2.3 The risks of demand letters

The major risk of demand letters is that they may lead to a termination/eviction notice. Another risk is that your identification of risks of special damages or of emotional distress may backfire. Here are two examples: By identifying valuable pieces of personal property, you may help your landlord enforce a money judgment against you in the future (if the item is not exempt from seizure — see chapter 7). Telling the landlord about the presence of an ailing parent may reveal a weakness of which a really unusual landlord will take advantage.

3. Building Inspections

Cities and counties have various staff whose jobs are to determine whether buildings meet code requirements. This book uses the term "building inspection" to include inspections by any or all of these officials — building inspectors, fire inspectors, health inspectors, electrical inspectors, etc. — except where it is important to distinguish among them.

Building inspections are often advisable (although, in many areas, not available) if a demand letter alone doesn't do the trick and you're not ready to give up. An inspection obtains an experienced and neutral expert's statement about the condition of your home. This kind of evidence may be important if you decide to use any of the rent-withholding defenses discussed in chapter 6, and the date of the inspector's notification to the landlord may be important in proving the landlord's attempted eviction is retaliatory.

Usually an inspection can be very helpful; however, there are risks. Occasionally, a building inspection will disclose such serious problems that the county or city will condemn the unit, sometimes very quickly. A related risk is that the landlord will be forced to fix something — such as door widths or ceiling heights — that you really don't care about, and then will have no money left over to do what you want done. Worse yet, the landlord may decide that compliance with a code provision that means nothing to you is too expensive. If the enforcing agency insists on compliance, the landlord may simply try to evict you. Although the retaliation defense discussed in chapter 8 may help, even retaliatory evictions are permitted if compliance with the codes "requires alteration, remodeling, or demolition, which would effectively deprive the tenant of the use of the dwelling unit for an extended period of time."

State law encourages counties and cities to use alternatives to condemnation, such as housing receivership programs, that allow tenants to keep living in their homes while the landlord is forced to make repairs. If your local government doesn't have such a policy in place, it's a good thing to talk about with local officials.

A few jurisdictions don't seem to "get it" that their job is to enforce safety for the sake of residents; in those jurisdictions inspectors may simply tell tenants to "move, or we will have to shut the house down" without even bothering to inspect, much less forcing the landlord to make needed repairs.

3.1 Code violations and the act

Not every violation of the building code is necessarily a violation of ORLTA. Some provisions of the act require that certain items comply with building codes when they are installed, and that they continue to function in good working order. For such items, the codes are relevant only to assess "good working order." Also, some code requirements, such as those requiring that ceilings be at least a certain height, often have nothing to do with habitability. On the other hand, safety from fire hazards may reasonably require complete fire code compliance, and water supply systems and sewage disposal systems must comply with the applicable codes to meet the requirements of the law.

Some code provisions may be enforceable by a tenant even if they are not covered by ORLTA. If, under a statute or code provision, a landlord has a duty concerning the premises, the landlord's violation of that duty may form the basis of a lawsuit against the landlord. If a court finds that you were within the class of persons the statute or code provisions were designed to protect, you should get damages if you can show that the landlord's violations caused you harm through no fault of your own. For example, if a code provision requires landlords to provide fire extinguishers, you should recover damages if you can show that the landlord didn't provide one and that a fire that you didn't start caused more damage to your belongings than it would have caused if a fire extinguisher had been readily available.

3.2 How to get an inspection

Although there are usually different inspectors for violations of building, electrical, plumbing, fire, and health codes, the usual procedure is for the building inspector to come first, and then to request electrical and/or plumbing inspections if they appear to be needed. If you are concerned only with an electrical or plumbing problem, or with fire or health code violations, you should ask for an appropriate inspection without going through the building inspector.

To arrange for a building inspection, look in the "Government" listings in your telephone book under the city you live in (or the county if you are not within city limits). In Portland, for example, there are listings under the Bureau of Buildings for building inspections, electrical permits and inspections, and plumbing permits and inspections. Some localities list sewage inspections separately from plumbing inspections. Fire inspections are obtained through the fire bureau, and health inspections through the county health department. In rural parts of the state, many of these inspection services may not be available.

Arranging for inspections outside a city or in a city without specific listings for these purposes may take a little more looking. Just remember that it is necessary to get a permit to do anything almost everywhere, and an inspector is at least theoretically available to ensure that the permit is appropriate and that it is complied with.

You should not have to pay for an inspection. It is the public duty of the various agencies to investigate alleged code violations and to enforce the relevant codes. Occasionally, however, you will run into an inspector who is not used to compliance inspections unrelated to a permit application and who doesn't like the idea of a mere tenant getting "something for nothing." Don't take a refusal for an answer; talk to a superior official and, if necessary, work your way up to the county commissioner or mayor. Sometimes a letter to the newspaper will get results. On the other hand, it may be worth a small fee to get the inspection done quickly and without a separate battle. Just make sure you record the name of the inspector and obtain a copy of the inspection report.

CHAPTER SIX

GETTING REPAIRS: WITHHOLDING RENT AND SUING THE LANDLORD

A tenant serious about repairs, but unable to get a landlord's attention to habitability problems by using a demand letter and/or a building inspection, has a few more options. The options will depend to some extent on the kind of problem the tenant is experiencing. In some situations, a tenant is not required to pay rent or is authorized to use part of the rent to cure problems caused by the landlord's violations of repair or maintenance obligations, or is even authorized to stay somewhere else until repairs are made. The act also gives a tenant the right to recover money damages for these and most other violations by the landlord.

Each of the remedies for tenants discussed in this chapter can be a defense or partial defense in an eviction case or a damage case started by a landlord. By withholding rent for habitability violations or using rent money to pay for repairs of "essential services" and then deducting the cost, a tenant can show either that no rent is due or that the amount due is less than that demanded in an eviction notice. The tenant can show he or she does not owe rent when asserting a retaliatory eviction defense in any kind of eviction case (see chapter 8), or in a damage case after the tenancy is done.

Although interrupting the flow of rent to the landlord is a powerful weapon in obtaining repairs, it is also the most likely way to end up in court fighting a retaliatory eviction ostensibly for nonpayment of rent.

1. Lack of Essential Services

ORLTA recognizes that some habitability requirements are "essential services" that deserve special protection (ORS 90.365). For a regular rental — in a house, apartment, or rented mobile home (not in a park) — essential services include hot and cold running water, gas and electricity, light fixtures, locks on outside doors, latches on windows, stoves and refrigerators either provided or promised by the landlord, and any other essential service that would prevent habitability violations. Habitability violations include anything that "creates a serious threat to the tenant's health, safety, or property or makes the dwelling unit unfit for occupancy" (ORS 90.100). In a floating or manufactured home facility, an essential service includes sewage disposal, water and electrical supplies, drainage systems required by law, and any other essential service that would prevent a "serious threat to the tenant's health, safety, or property."

If a tenant is facing a habitability problem that meets the above definition (e.g., a broken furnace in the winter, a dead refrigerator, E. coli in the water supply, a collapsing ceiling, etc.), there are five possible solutions. Four require advance written notice about the problem, with the tenant then giving the landlord a reasonable time and reasonable access to fix the problem (ORS 90.365). The type and seriousness of the problem determine what is a "reasonable time." The following are the four solutions that require advance written notice:

(a) Terminate the rental agreement on 48 hours' written notice if the problem is due to the landlord's intentional or negligent conduct and poses an "imminent and serious threat" to health, safety, or property of the tenant and the landlord fails to make the repair within that time. "Imminent and serious" does not mean possible harm that could come from radon, lead-based paint, asbestos, or the risk of flooding or earthquake. The landlord's failure to fix the problem is "intentional or negligent" only if the landlord does not substantially supply the essential service after being notified or doesn't make a reasonable effort to supply it so long as the failure to supply isn't beyond the landlord's control. Note: The notice must say what the problem is and that the repair will keep the tenancy from terminating.

(b) "Repair and deduct" from future rent the cost of having the repair of an essential service done in a workmanlike manner, or the value of the tenant's doing a workmanlike repair, after the landlord's failure to provide the essential service. If the lack of the service poses an imminent and serious threat to the health or safety of the tenants or danger to the tenant's property, the landlord's failure to fix the problem does not have to be intentional or negligent before this remedy is available. For nonemergency situations, though, "intentional or negligent" applies.

The tenant must submit receipts or an itemized statement for the repair, making and keeping copies. If the work is done by a licensed professional, the maximum deduction is $1,000 to fix problems that are imminent and serious threats to health, safety, or property. If the situation is less urgent, or if the repair is made by someone who is not a licensed professional, the maximum is $500. The landlord can agree to reimburse for a repair that costs more than these amounts; he or she can also specify who will do the work. (If you think the repairs will exceed the $500 limit, you should obtain written authorization before proceeding with the repairs [see Sample 8].)

The required advance notice period varies for "repair and deduct." If the problem is in the "imminent and serious" category, the notice can be verbal first, so long as it is followed right away with written notice. Both kinds of notice must give the landlord at least 48 hours to fix the problem. If the problem is a broken stove or refrigerator, the advance written notice must be at least 72 hours. For other essential services, the notice must be at least seven days. Notices that are sent by regular mail get an extra three days' mailing time before these time periods start.

(c) Seek a reasonable amount of substitute services, deducting tenants' actual and reasonable cost from future rent. Examples are the purchase and use of space heaters when a furnace breaks down, and the purchase of bottled water if the water in the rental is not safe to drink. Again, the landlord's failure to supply the essential services has to be intentional or negligent.

SAMPLE 8
WRITTEN PERMISSION TO EXCEED
$500 LIMIT

June 1, 20--

To Mr. Tenant, of 123 Tenant Lane, Portland, Oregon:

I hereby authorize you to spend up to $875 to obtain the following repairs and to deduct the actual cost of those repairs, up to that amount, from future rent payments: repair or replacement of hot water heater as needed, replacement of rotted shower stall in downstairs bathroom.

Mary Smith

Mary Smith

(Landlord)

(d) Seek substitute housing during the noncompliance, getting excused under ORLTA from paying rent until the place can be lived in again, and seek the actual and reasonable cost or reasonable value of substitute housing. Substitute housing is an available remedy only if the landlord's intentional or negligent failure to provide an essential service makes the dwelling unsafe or unfit to occupy until repairs are made. The landlord can be liable for substitute housing costs only to the level of the cost or value of housing comparable to that of the rental in habitable condition.

If the tenant decides to use one of these options in an emergency, he or she can attempt to give "actual notice," then follow it up as soon as possible with the required written notice. If there is a written rental agreement, that agreement may require additional kinds of notice, such as facsimile or e-mail (ORS 90.150, ORS 90.155).

The fifth choice is to seek money damages based on the reduction ("diminution") in rental value of the premises caused by the loss of essential services. For this option, the landlord needn't have been deliberately or grossly negligent. Nor does the tenant have to make written demand, although the tenant would be smart to put the demand in writing: in court, proving that the demand was made has as much significance as making the demand itself.

All of the repair remedies can be used to justify rent withholding if they are properly used. Each can defeat an eviction based on nonpayment of rent by showing that all or part of the rent wasn't due. Each can be used in any kind of eviction action as part of a retaliatory eviction defense to show that the tenant did not owe rent (see chapter 8).

Remedies (b) and (c) allow the tenant to get the repairs made if the landlord refuses to perform them. The major strength of the essential service remedies is that they take a lot of the risk out of measuring the amount of damages. Unlike the "recoupment and counterclaim" remedy, which requires a rather crude estimate of the cash value of the landlord's violations, the essential service remedies ordinarily enable the tenant (and the court) to compute precisely the amount of rent that is not due.

The tenant cannot use this section of the law if the loss of services was caused by a deliberate or negligent act or omission by the tenant or someone in the tenant's household or present as a guest of the tenant. For example, this section cannot be used to force the landlord to pay a utility bill for which the tenant is responsible.

1.1 The risks

The essential service remedies have some limitations. One is that, unless the "essential service" the tenant wants the landlord to supply is listed in the statute ORS 90.100(10), it is unclear what constitutes an essential service. The second risk is that a tenant's rights under the essential service section depend on how a court applies such dangerously ambiguous terms as "grossly negligent" and "reasonable." Of course, both parties may want to avoid the risks of ambiguity in court by agreeing beforehand on a repair schedule that may or may not include the same remedies as those listed in the essential service section.

Finally, a tenant cannot use both the repair or substitution remedies of the essential service section and the more general remedies provided by ORS 90.360: injunction, damages, and/or termination of the tenancy (all of which are discussed later in this chapter).

The impact of this limitation may vary. It may mean that a tenant who wishes to use the repair and deduct remedy for an electrical failure may have to give up any right to recover special damages for the loss of food spoiled in a freezer because of that failure. On the other hand, the tenant can recover special damages under the "recoupment and counterclaim" approach for essential services (see below) without losing the right to the ORS 90.360 remedies (injunction, damages, and/or termination) for other problems. And if the landlord's violation was "willful" under ORS 90.375 (a term that should include "deliberate" violations and may include "grossly negligent" ones), the tenant has the choice of injunction, double damages, and/or termination. (See chapter 7 on lockouts and utility shutoffs.)

In addition to these general limitations, each of the essential service remedies has its own peculiar risks, described below.

2. Substitute Services

The substitute services remedy of ORS 90.365 permits tenants to procure "reasonable amounts of the essential service during the period of the landlord's noncompliance and deduct their actual and reasonable cost from the rent." Sample 9 is an example of a substitute-service notice.

Sometimes calculating "reasonable amounts" is simple and sometimes it is not.

If the landlord had agreed in a written rental contract to pay the electric bills but stopped, this remedy permits the tenant to sign up for the utility service after the appropriate notice to the landlord. The tenant should be able to deduct from the rent the "actual and reasonable cost" of the service. The landlord may claim that the tenant took advantage of the situation to consume more of the service than would normally be consumed by that household or a household of that size. In addition, some utilities require a substantial deposit. The landlord may dispute that the payment of the deposit was an actual and reasonable cost of obtaining the service.

Tenants who use this remedy should attach copies of the relevant receipts along with an explanation with each rent payment that is reduced by the use of this remedy. Tenants must keep the original receipts and copies of their letters.

SAMPLE 9
LETTER THREATENING SUBSTITUTE SERVICE REMEDY

October 20, 20--

Dear Ms. Smith:

I am your tenant at 123 Tenant Lane. Under our rental agreement, you are responsible for supplying and paying for electricity for my home. I just learned that you have not paid the bill for over two months; the power company says it will turn off the electricity on November 15, 20--, if the bill is not paid.

If you have not taken care of the bill before November 15, 20--, I will open an account in my own name and deduct the amount of any required deposit and each month's electric charges from future rent.

I.M. Tenant

I.M. Tenant

Sometimes there are external problems that keep this solution from working. For example, some kinds of utilities may be unwilling or even unable to contract with someone other than the owner for service. Another situation may be that the utility meter serves more than one dwelling unit, and the tenant would have to pay everyone's bill.

A similar problem arises when, for example, a furnace breaks down. Although this remedy would seem to permit a tenant to purchase or rent an electric heater for each major room, electric heaters draw an enormous amount of electric current and often lead to blown fuses. They are extremely dangerous if used with oversized fuses and they can cause a fire by overloading the electrical circuits or by igniting flammable material that is placed too close to the heating element. Tenants should ask the electric company or a building inspector about the capabilities of the wiring. The tenants should also shop around for heaters and compare the cost of renting to buying, and even compare these costs with the costs of staying somewhere else if the problem occurs during cold weather. The landlord may argue that the more expensive approach was not "reasonable," and it helps to be in a position to prove there was no choice or that the cost differences were not significant. The tenants should make and keep notes of conversations with stores, inspectors, the utility service, and possible substitute housing.

3. Substitute Housing

The substitute housing remedy of ORS 90.365 permits a tenant to move out temporarily, to stop paying the rent, and to recover the "fair and reasonable value of reasonably comparable substitute housing," but only when the tenant can show the landlord intentionally or negligently failed to provide the service. Factors such as available transportation, location, and availability of choices are all relevant in determining when substitute housing is "reasonably comparable" to the tenant's usual rented home.

The "fair and reasonable value" alternative is designed to benefit a tenant who receives free temporary housing from a friend or relative; the landlord is still liable to the tenant for the value of the substitute housing up to the amount of the monthly rent.

For example, you move into your great-aunt's apartment because your furnace broke down in January during a cold spell. Your great-aunt may not demand any rent from you, but the court would be entitled to award you an amount that is representative of the fair and reasonable value of your substitute housing. Thus, if your aunt normally paid $600 per month for rent, and you shared the apartment for a month, you might receive an award of $300, for this would be the fair and reasonable value of your substitute housing.

The tenant's ability to both stop paying the rent and recover the cost or value of the substitute housing is necessary to give landlords an incentive to make repairs. Otherwise, a landlord unwilling to make repairs might simply do nothing, treating a tenancy as having ended when it hasn't. Sample 10 is an example of what to send a landlord in this situation; the tenant must state clearly that the tenant is not terminating the rental agreement or abandoning the premises when leaving the property. (An abandonment would allow the landlord to treat the lease or rental agreement as ended.)

SAMPLE 10
NOTIFICATION OF SUBSTITUTE HOUSING REMEDY

November 11, 20--

Dear Ms. Smith:

I am your tenant at 123 Tenant Lane, Portland, Oregon. As you recall, I both called and wrote you on November 3, 20-- to ask you to repair the roof at my home because the ceiling in the bedroom had collapsed from leaking water and the ceiling in the living room was beginning to sag from the weight of rainwater.

You have done nothing to fix the problem. These conditions are dangerous. For that reason, I am going to find temporary substitute housing, where I will be moving tomorrow. I am not giving up my right to possession of the rental. I will withhold further rent until I can live in the rental again. Furthermore, I want to be reimbursed for reasonable costs of my temporary housing.

I.M. Tenant

I.M. Tenant

3.1 The risks

Theoretically, this remedy puts significant financial pressure on the landlord. The main problem with the remedy is that the tenant has to move, which is a burden that is rarely worthwhile. A lawsuit against the landlord may accomplish more. Once in a while, though, a tenant who has already started a lawsuit may have to leave temporarily if conditions get significantly worse while the case is underway, so this step would be a necessary part of the move process.

4. Repair and Deduct

This essential service remedy allows a tenant to pay for the necessary repairs and to deduct the cost from the rent. Note that repair and deduct remedies are available only for essential service problems (including broken stoves and refrigerators), as discussed at the start of this chapter. Remember that this is the one essential service remedy for which mere negligence on the part of the landlord is sufficient; "gross negligence" or a deliberate act on the part of the landlord is not necessary. The minimum notice time and the maximum deductible dollar amounts vary, as mentioned above.

A conscientious landlord who hears about a lacking essential service will sometimes agree to have the tenant deal with the problem and deduct the costs from future rent. It is a good idea for the tenant to confirm such an agreement in writing. Some landlords will agree to a reduction higher than the statutory amount if the repair will cost more than that amount; the landlord should make the limit clear in writing. The tenant should also insist on getting a clear written authorization, to avoid misunderstanding.

Samples 11, 12, and 13 are examples of notices designed for a typical repair and deduct situation. Not following the statute precisely can prevent the use of this remedy successfully as a defense to an eviction. If the landlord specified the person who was to do the work, the tenant should confirm that the specified person did the work.

There are two major risks involved with the repair and deduct remedy. First, it seems so practical that many tenants use it without advance notice to the landlord or for reasons not covered by the repair-and-deduct law. Second, there is always the risk that the work will not be done properly or that the landlord will claim the property has been damaged by poor repairs. For this reason, it is safest to encourage the landlord to exercise the right to specify a repair person. Know, however, that the landlord's choice may not be available for under the dollar amounts the statute permits.

Ideally, the tenant will get several estimates and get the landlord to agree to one of them in writing. Most professional repair people are bonded, so the landlord should be satisfied that a responsible party stands behind the work. The tenant should also try to get the landlord to agree in writing to the use of a nonprofessional when that is an option so that the landlord can't later claim that the choice was negligent.

SAMPLE 11
NOTICE OF REPAIR AND DEDUCT REMEDY

May 15, 20--

Dear Mr. Smith:

I am your tenant at 123 Tenant Lane, Portland, Oregon. I called both your office and home phone numbers today to notify you that my water heater, which I previously informed you was leaking, has now broken down entirely. I have no hot water at all for cooking or cleaning, doing laundry, or bathing myself or my children.

The law permits me to have a new water heater installed and to deduct the expense, up to $500, from the rent. You may agree to allow me to exceed the $500 limit. In the alternative, you may opt to have the repair made yourself, so long as you do so within seven days *(ten days if letter is mailed)* after the date of this letter.

Unless you have the repair made within that time, I hereby give you notice that I will purchase a water heater, have it installed by a licensed plumber, and deduct the total cost up to $500 from next month's rent.

To discuss how you want to proceed, please call me at (555) 555-5555 or (555) 555-4444.

I.M. Tenant

I.M. Tenant

5. Recoupment and Counterclaim

The recoupment and counterclaim remedies are probably the most useful tools a tenant has under the law for dealing with repair problems. Either may justify a tenant's refusal to pay at least part of the rent when a landlord violates obligations under the act or under the rental agreement. They both can help a tenant show that no rent was due in a nonpayment of rent eviction and can defend the tenant from a retaliatory eviction.

REPAIR AND DEDUCT NOTICE
(AFTER YOU HAVE HAD REPAIRS MADE)

June 1, 20--

Dear Mr. Smith:

Enclosed are a check for $150 and a copy of a receipt for $450 for the purchase and installation of a water heater at 123 Tenant Street. As I notified you in my letter of May 15, 20--, the old water heater, which had been leaking and which you knew about already, stopped working completely. You did not replace it and did not specify anyone to repair it within 48 hours after I left the notice at 1234 Broke Street (address designated in rental agreement), so I hired Ace Plumbing to do the work. This month's rent of $600 is therefore paid in full.

If you dispute the amount of the deduction or my right to do this, please let me know in writing right away.

Sincerely,

I.M. Tenant

I.M. Tenant

enclosure (optional) — copy of ORS 90.365

Both remedies work on the principle that the landlord may owe the tenant "damages" for violation of the landlord's obligations under ORLTA or under the rental agreement.

Counterclaiming is a complicated procedure; many tenants who attempt to counterclaim without the help of a lawyer do so unsuccessfully.

5.1 Damages

ORS 90.360(2) entitles a tenant to "damages" for a landlord's violation of the rental agreement or of the habitability section of the act. ORS 90.125 entitles either party to "appropriate damages" for almost any violation of ORLTA.

"Damages" are simply the monetary value of the harm caused by a wrong, even if it's hard to assess the amount. "General damages" for a landlord's violation of habitability obligations are measured by the reduction in rental value of the premises caused by that violation. From a landlord's point of view, general damages caused by a tenant's violations may be measured by a decrease in rental value of the premises. "Special damages" are peculiar to each situation, as when a tenant's furniture is harmed by a water leak. Usually, the cost of repairing the furniture or the fair market value of the furniture at the time of the harm (whichever is smaller) would be special damages that might be added to the general damages (reduced rental value) caused by the leak.

The act also specifies some "statutory damages." These are minimum amounts that must or may be awarded for certain kinds of violations. The purposes of such provisions are to deter others from committing violations and to ensure that an injured party will recover something even when it's hard to prove or to measure damages. For example, one statutory damage provision permits an award of up to twice the actual damages or twice the monthly rent (whichever is greater) as a sanction against retaliatory evictions.

If a tenant has a right to any kind of damages because of a landlord's violations of ORLTA or of the rental agreement, ORS 90.125 and ORS 90.360(2) provide that the tenant may respond to a landlord's lawsuit with claims for recoupment and counterclaim, or can file his or her own lawsuit.

5.2 The remedies

"Recoupment" is the process by which debts between two parties cancel each other out, in whole or in part, if the debts arose out of the same transaction. "Same transaction" in the landlord and tenant relationship covers all of the relations between the landlord and the tenant that arise because of the tenancy.

In a landlord and tenant relationship, recoupment means a tenant can use the landlord's violations of ORLTA or of the rental agreement to show that unpaid rent was not really owed. If the tenant stops paying rent, regardless of the reason, he or she may show that all or part of the rent wasn't due under the concept of recoupment because he or she is entitled to damages for the landlord's failure, for example, to fix a toilet. The major question is the amount of damages to which the tenant is entitled.

The great value of recoupment is that, so long as the right of the tenant is one for which damages are appropriate, and so long as the violation was not the tenant's fault, recoupment should be available. There are no complicated notice requirements or waiting periods, although a notice of some kind is always advisable (see chapter 5). Of course, tenants, just like their landlords, must always act in good faith and "mitigate" (minimize) their damages.

Another advantage of recoupment is that the tenant doesn't have to spend the rent money on substitute housing or repairing the rental in order to use recoupment as a defense against an eviction for nonpayment of rent. That means that the tenant who ultimately chooses to move can spend his or her money on moving expenses and then use the recoupment defense if the landlord sues later, claiming back rent.

An example: You pay rent for many months even though your landlord hasn't responded to your requests for heat and for repairs to a leaky roof. As the weather gets colder and wetter, you finally stop paying rent and the landlord tries to evict you. You can defend the eviction action by claiming that the damages to which you are entitled for the landlord's violations equal or exceed any amount the landlord claims as rent. You don't have to show that you applied any of the rent to repairs or services. If you move out before the landlord tries to evict you, and the landlord sues you for unpaid rent, you can use the same approach to show that all or part of the rent claimed is not due.

While a recoupment can show that all or part of the rent claimed by a landlord is not really due, a counterclaim by a tenant may result in a judgment for damages against a landlord in either an eviction or a case for back rent. For example, a tenant can respond to an eviction action by counterclaiming for the same kinds of things that a tenant can seek by filing an independent lawsuit, including an order that repairs be made.

For example: You stop paying rent. Your landlord serves you with a 72-hour notice (a kind of notice usually appropriate for nonpayment of rent) and starts an eviction case against you. If you defend by saying that all of the rent claimed is offset by the damages the landlord owes you because the toilet hasn't worked for six weeks, that's a recoupment. If you say your damages are greater than the amount of rent claimed and ask that the court award you a judgment for the difference (and/or an order that the landlord fix the toilet), you are asserting a counterclaim.

To use the recoupment or counterclaim remedies, the tenant will have to show the extent of the hardship imposed by the landlord's violations. Two examples: lack of heat undoubtedly reduces rental value more in winter than in summer; therefore, general damages for lack of heat in January should be much greater than those for lack of heat in August. A leak in the ceiling of a spare room likely will not be as significant as a leak in the ceiling over the tenant's bed.

5.3 How to use the remedies

The tenant who plans to use the recoupment and counterclaim defenses must decide first whether to withhold all or part of the rent, depending on the nature and extent of the landlord's breaches and the hardship they have caused. Next, there must be notice to the landlord (see Sample 13). Then the tenant must show that he or she is truly withholding the rent. A good way to do this is to open a special savings account in the tenant's name and deposit every cent of the withheld rent into that account as the rent becomes due. The only exception would be for expenses that are absolutely necessary and caused by the landlord's breaches. For such expenses, the tenant should keep meticulous records and all receipts. Paying rent into a savings account as it becomes due shows the tenant's good faith and can dispel any notion that the tenant simply doesn't have the rent money to pay. In addition, the court may require the tenant to pay that rent money into court.

It is not a good idea to spend the withheld money on repairs as this will make it difficult to estimate the amount of damages suffered as a result of a landlord's breach. There is also the possibility that the tenant will end up moving after having fixed someone else's property. The tenant may also need this money to cover moving expenses if he or she decides to move.

The final step in using the recoupment or counterclaim remedies is to keep track of every added expense and inconvenience caused by the landlord's violations of the act or of the rental agreement. This record will be useful in negotiating with the landlord or in presenting the case in court. If the landlord agrees to make

SAMPLE 13
NOTICE THAT YOU ARE WITHHOLDING RENT
DUE TO LANDLORD'S BREACHES

January 15, 20--

Dear Ms. Smith:

This letter follows my letter to you of December 1, 20--, and our six phone conversations during the past two months, in which I requested the following repairs:

- Broken furnace

- Leaking roof

- Blocked toilet

- Defective kitchen wiring

I also sent you a copy of a city building department report about these problems. Despite the seriousness of these problems, you have done nothing to remedy them.

Beginning immediately, I will withhold my entire monthly rent until you have made substantial progress toward repair of these problems. If you still refuse to comply, I will pursue all of my legal remedies under the Landlord and Tenant Act.

I.M. Tenant

I.M. Tenant

repairs, the parties should write a settlement agreement as discussed in chapter 5. It is wise for both sides to get independent advice from a lawyer before signing. If the landlord doesn't give in, the tenant must consider going to court before the landlord does (as discussed below). (See chapter 8 for information on evictions.)

5.4 The risks

5.4a Recoupment

The major drawback of recoupment is that there is no exact measure for damages. The judge or jury gets to decide how much to award the tenant in damages for the landlord's violations.

5.4b Counterclaims and the right of redemption

One of the most unusual provisions of ORLTA is that it allows a judge to order a tenant to pay into court all or part of the rent claimed by the landlord as a condition of being allowed to assert a counterclaim. This is often referred to as the "rent-into-court" or "redemption" provision. It does not apply to recoupment or to other defenses; it does not apply in claims for rent when the tenant has moved out; and it should not apply to eviction actions that are not based on nonpayment of rent. If a judge orders a tenant to pay rent into court for any reason other than to raise a counterclaim, a tenant who cannot pay it should get legal advice immediately to consider the possibility of an emergency appeal of the judge's ruling — a ruling that will most likely result in an eviction.

Although the rent-into-court provision effectively charges the tenant for a day in court, it has a positive side, which is — if the tenant can afford it — well worth the price. The tenant who pays rent into court is entitled to pay any amount still owing to the landlord if the court finds that the amount paid into court is not enough to cover the rent that is owed. If the amount paid into court is enough to cover any rent found due, or if the tenant makes up any difference after the trial and before judgment is entered, the tenant wins the case and can keep living in the rental.

This "second chance" or "redemption" provision takes the risk out of estimating damages. Even if the court decides the tenant should get a smaller amount of damages for the landlord's violations than the tenant had estimated, the rent-into-court provision will give the tenant a second chance to prevent eviction for nonpayment of rent.

For example: You paid $450 monthly rent for several months, even though the landlord has refused to fix the heater. Now you have stopped paying rent and instead spent $179.50 to have the heater fixed. The landlord has brought an eviction action for nonpayment of rent. This time, instead of merely relying on the recoupment defense, you file a counterclaim in the eviction action. You ask for $179.50 for fixing the heater and $400 for the reduction in rental value of the premises over the entire period of time for which you had to go without heat. The landlord then asks the court to make you pay all of the $450 he or she claims as rent into court. You argue that you will probably win your counterclaim and show the judge the receipt. The judge makes you pay $250 into court. At the trial, if the judge or a jury decides you are entitled to only $100 damages for your lack of heat, the result will be that the landlord will get the $250 already paid into court, but you will have the choice of paying an additional $100 to make up the entire balance due, and then be able to stay. The ability to "win" the case by paying the $100 in this illustration may determine whether the court awards attorney fees and court costs to you or against you. It may be worth it to pay the $100 even if you have decided to move.

Obviously, the tenant would win if the amount paid into court was equal to or greater than the amount of rent the court found due to the landlord. Also, if the tenant wins the counterclaim so that the landlord owes the money, the court will release the money paid into court to the tenant — as part of the money the landlord owes to the tenant. Finally, if the court finds that the damages suffered by the tenant equal the amount of rent paid into court, that money too will be paid to the tenant.

Attorneys who regularly represent tenants often have their clients pay rent into court without waiting for the landlord to ask for an order, and landlords' attorneys may decide not to ask for rent to be paid into court for fear of losing the case on the basis of the redemption provision.

A tenant who is defending against eviction has very little chance to get a delay in the trial, although a landlord can agree to a delay and can ask for a delay to prepare his or her own case. In such a situation, the tenant may be required to pay rent into court to get a delay in the trial date. Rent paid into court for a delay may not give the tenant a "second chance" the way that rent paid into court to support a counterclaim does; a tenant seeking a delay should generally counterclaim if he or she has grounds.

Getting the assistance of a lawyer is extremely important for the tenant who decides to counterclaim; the procedure is complicated.

6. Suing the Landlord

Everyone has heard the contention that the best defense is a strong offense. This premise holds true in landlord-tenant disputes, too. Tenants often fare better as plaintiffs filing a lawsuit against the landlord than as defendants in an eviction case. A tenant with substantial complaints concerning a landlord's violations of a rental agreement or of the act may file a complaint in regular court for the following reasons:

(a) Protection against eviction until the case is over

(b) Protection against any retaliatory action

(c) Damages for the landlord's violations of the act or of the rental agreement

(d) An order that the landlord make repairs, and, where appropriate, an order that the landlord refrain from making unlawful entries or from attempting to evict the tenant through lockouts and utility shutoffs (see chapter 7)

(e) A declaration fixing the rent due in the future at a reduced amount until repairs are completed

(f) Damages under the Unlawful Trade and Unlawful Debt Collection Practices Acts

(g) A finding that the landlord is liable to the tenant for the tenant's attorney fees and court costs

(h) Any other relief the court deems appropriate

For a tenant, the advantages of being a plaintiff are many. There is less chance of ending up on a tenant "blacklist." The court is less likely to believe that the tenant made things up as an excuse not to pay the rent. Also, the landlord and his or her attorney are more likely to have a realistic discussion of the possible outcome and expense of the case than if they assume they are dealing with a routine eviction.

Moreover, for a variety of reasons, things go more slowly when the tenant is the plaintiff, so there is more time for adequate preparation than in the speedy procedure provided for evictions. The plaintiff can sue for any relief he or she is entitled to, while counterclaims in an eviction action are limited to claims arising under ORLTA, the rental agreement, or certain consumer protection laws. However, having an attorney for an affirmative case is essential.

TABLE 1
REPAIR REMEDIES AND THEIR LIMITATIONS

	Demand letters	Building inspections	Substitute services	Substitute housing	Repair and deduct	Dependent convenants	Recoupment	Counterclaims	Suing the landlord
KINDS OF PROBLEMS									
Habitability violations ORS 90.320	X	X				X	X	X	X
Essential services	X	X	X	X	X	X	X	X	X
Other violations of the act	X						X	X	X
Violations of the rental agreement	X						X	X	X
LIMITATIONS									
Written notice to landlord required	X		X	X	X				
Landlord's act must be negligent					X				
Landlord's act must be deliberate or grossly negligent			X	X					
Remedy is complicated to use			X	X	X				X
Measure of damages is imprecise							X	X	X
Tenant may have to pay rent into court								X	X

If the tenant asks the court to order the landlord not to bring a separate eviction action or not to engage in unlawful "self-help" eviction attempts, the landlord will probably ask that the court require an "undertaking." The undertaking is usually in the form of a promise by a bonding company or a financially solvent individual to pay the landlord all losses if and when it is determined that the court's order should not have been made. On the other hand, there are statutes that permit the court to require the payment of money into court instead of an undertaking.

Most such court orders are not effective unless there is an undertaking or its equivalent, and the result of the rent-into-court equivalent is a perfectly proper, court-sanctioned rent strike with obvious financial implications for the landlord. An exception is that no undertaking should be necessary if the tenant is seeking an order that the landlord refrain from violating the act's prohibitions against lockouts, utility shutoffs, and invasions of privacy (see chapter 7).

Once the court orders at the actual trial that the landlord make repairs or refrain from bringing a retaliatory eviction, there is no longer any need for an undertaking.

6.1 How to use the remedy

If your landlord has really "done you wrong," if you have tried everything else, and if you are ready for a long fight to enforce your right to decent housing, filing a lawsuit is probably the way to go. Keep all your records, estimate your damages accurately (being very specific), find an attorney as discussed in chapter 15, and see your landlord in court!

6.2 The risks

There are disadvantages to filing a lawsuit. Suing your landlord requires much more energy on the part of your attorney than does defending an eviction action. It is, therefore, more difficult to get a legal aid attorney to do it and more expensive to hire your own attorney.

It also requires more of your own time and energy. Many tenants will settle for a period of free rent, perhaps some cash, and adequate time to move, after having originally hoped for an order for repairs and a long-term lease in return for past damages. You will do better than most tenants, but unless you have exceptional endurance you will settle for something quite different from what you originally wanted. This result is typical in all kinds of civil litigation: well over 90 percent of all cases are settled before trial on terms that neither side would have accepted when the case was first filed.

7. Comparing the Remedies

Table 1 compares the coverage and limitations of each of the remedies, but make sure you read chapters 5 and 6 to understand them fully. For example, repair and deduct is available only for essential services, but the discussion of this remedy shows how essential services may include many conditions that also violate the provisions of the habitability section of the law (ORS 90.320).

All of the remedies discussed in chapter 5 and this chapter are available to tenants acting together as well as to a tenant struggling alone. Tenants of the same landlord who are living in deplorable conditions may benefit from concerted action (see chapter 15).

8. Hazardous Conditions/Posted Premises

Occasionally a health and safety agency will post a notice on a dwelling declaring it unfit to occupy because of conditions at the premises. A tenant usually will vacate the "posted" premises because of the hazard, which sometimes is caused by neglect or misuse by the landlord or by the tenant, or even by acts of nature. ORS 90.380 describes the rights and duties of each party when an agency takes this kind of action. ORS 90.380 also describes the roles of each party when an agency has notified a landlord about health and safety violations the landlord needs to fix in order to prevent the posting of the property.

An agency concerned about a health or safety problem at a dwelling should notify not only the landlord but also the tenant about the problem. Unfortunately, that doesn't always happen, especially if there is frequent tenant turnover. The rights of the tenant in these situations will depend to some extent on how much the tenant knows.

If an agency notifies a landlord that a unit is unlawful (but not technically unsafe) to occupy because of conditions that violate the law and "materially affect" health or safety, the current tenant may stay in the unit but a new tenant cannot move in until the landlord fixes the problem. The existing tenant may or may not be experiencing problems that violate the habitability requirements of ORLTA. If the agency has pointed out the same problems to the landlord that the tenant has, however, the tenant's claims later for damages, recoupment, and perhaps counterclaims will be bolstered by the independent record of the landlord's awareness of the problem.

An unscrupulous landlord under notice from an agency not to enter into a new agreement may decide to get a new tenant anyway without disclosing to him or her the agency's notice. If that happens, and the new tenant finds out, he or she can recover the greater of two month's rent or actual damages. To keep dishonest landlords from claiming they disclosed the posting when they did not, the law requires this kind of disclosure to be in writing, to describe the condition, and to state that the landlord has a duty to correct the problem before entering into the new agreement. The disclosure must have a copy of the agency notice attached to it. The disclosure doesn't waive the new tenant's right to sue for unhabitable conditions; nor does it stop the government agency from posting the place or charging the landlord with penalties when it finds out the landlord has rented the place in violation of ORS 90.380.

The landlord cannot accept a "hold" deposit from the prospective tenant without this disclosure, either. If the landlord doesn't correct the problems before the applicant moves in or charges a "hold" deposit without disclosing, the applicant can sue for twice the amount of the deposit or $100 under ORS 90.297. The landlord has 14 days within which to return the deposit, security deposits, and prepaid rent. The applicant or new tenant can and probably should report the offending landlord to the agency as well.

Similar rules apply for dwellings that actually have been posted as unlawful and unsafe to occupy. If a government agency has posted a place as both "unlawful" and "unsafe," the landlord may not rent it without correcting the conditions that led to the posting. If the landlord knowingly rents a posted dwelling, the tenant need give the landlord only actual (verbal) notice of the termination and the reason for the termination. (It is best to use or follow up with written notice, of course.) The landlord has 14 days to return all deposits and prepaid rent prorated to the later of the end of the tenant's notice period or the tenant's actual move-out date. Whether or not the tenant terminates, he or she is entitled to twice the actual damages sustained as a result of the unlawful rental or twice the monthly rent, whichever is greater. A tenant who knows a building has been posted but stays there anyway may be vulnerable not only to health or safety hazards, but also to a citation or arrest for trespass for violating the agency order.

If a governmental agency posts the dwelling as unlawful and unsafe to occupy because of such conditions when a tenant is already living there, and the tenant didn't cause the conditions, the tenant may immediately terminate with actual notice of the termination and the reason. The landlord has 14 days to return all deposits and prepaid rent. The tenant is entitled to the larger of either two months' periodic rent or twice the tenant's actual damages if the landlord knowingly allows the tenancy to continue.

If a governmental agency posts the dwelling as unlawful and unsafe to occupy and the condition was not caused by the landlord or the landlord's failure to maintain the unit, the landlord may terminate the tenancy on 24 hours' written notice giving the reason. If the tenant remains, the landlord can then initiate eviction proceedings.

Even if the dwelling is not posted, conditions at the outset of the tenancy that were not caused by the tenant and that pose an imminent and serious threat to the health or safety of occupants within six months of the beginning of the tenancy give the tenant the right to immediately terminate with actual notice of the termination and the reason. The landlord has only four days in which to return all deposits and prepaid rent. If the landlord knew or "reasonably should have known" of the conditions, the tenant is entitled to twice the actual damages sustained as a result of the "violation" (presumably the hazardous conditions) or twice the monthly rent, whichever is greater — whether or not the tenant terminates.

In all of these situations, the tenant or applicant may tell the landlord in the notice of termination to mail the money by first-class mail to a specific address (which becomes the tenant's "last known address") or, in the alternative, have it ready for the tenant at the landlord's customary place of business (presumably during normal business hours). If the tenant does not state a choice, the landlord must mail the money (within the 4-day or 14-day period) to the tenant's last known address. A landlord who fails to return money that is due to a tenant under this section of the law is liable for twice the amount otherwise due.

CHAPTER SEVEN

LOCKOUTS, UTILITY SHUTOFFS, INVASIONS OF PRIVACY, AND SEIZURES OF TENANTS' BELONGINGS

This chapter deals with lockouts, utility shutoffs, invasions of a tenant's privacy, and seizures of a tenant's belongings during the course of a tenancy. (Chapters 11 and 13 deal with belongings left behind at the end of a tenancy.) The problems discussed in this chapter have three things in common: they involve illegal conduct on the part of the landlord, the police probably won't help, and the tenant will need a lawyer if the landlord doesn't back down.

1. Lockouts and Utility Shutoffs

A lockout occurs when the landlord changes the locks or otherwise removes or excludes the tenant from the premises by force; a utility shutoff occurs when a landlord "willfully diminishes services to the tenant" (ORLTA 90.375). With one narrow exception described later in this chapter, both are unlawful.

Police rarely help tenants whose landlords have locked them out or shut off their power, believing such disputes to be "civil" rather than "criminal" in nature. Most police departments do recognize that tenants have the right to break into the premises from which they have been wrongfully excluded. If you find you must do this, use the least destructive means necessary. It is a good idea to have a witness present. If the landlord tries to stop you from re-entering your home, it is appropriate to call the police — they do intervene to keep people from being criminally assaulted.

Occasionally, a landlord may attempt to convince the police that there was never a rental agreement and that the tenant is a trespasser or a "squatter" — someone living there that neither the landlord nor the last tenant authorized to live there. It should be enough for the tenant to show the police a rent receipt or any other evidence of the tenancy such as utility bills addressed to the tenant or correspondence from the landlord. The tenant could even do something like describe the contents of the middle drawer of the bedroom dresser to show possession.

If your landlord removes or excludes you, seriously attempts or threatens unlawfully to do so, or "willfully" diminishes or interrupts your utility services to get rid of you, ORLTA gives you the option of terminating the tenancy or asking a court for an order that restrains the landlord from violating your rights and awards you statutory damages (see chapter 6). Statutory damages, in this case, are up to twice your actual damages or twice the monthly rent, whichever is greater.

Since emotional distress is often a legitimate and substantial portion of actual damages under such circumstances, the economic consequences may be disastrous for a landlord who violates these provisions. A tenant need not terminate the tenancy or ask for a court order to be entitled to damages in a case later.

Even if a landlord's behavior in causing a loss of utility service is not quite so serious as to be deemed willful, you may have self-help remedies under the essential service section of ORLTA if the behavior is at least "negligent." Under that section of the law, you may even be able to deduct the cost of restoring the utility service from your rent. In any event, you may have rights to a court order and damages under the general provisions of the act even if the landlord wasn't negligent (see chapter 6).

There is one exception to the rule against lockouts. This exception applies to rental agreements in which one tenant is the victim of a sexual assault, stalking, or domestic violence crime perpetrated by another tenant in the same unit. If one of the co-tenants informs the landlord that he or she is the victim of one of these crimes and asks the landlord to change the locks to the rental to exclude the other tenant, the landlord is obliged to do so or to allow the tenant to do so, at the tenant's expense. The landlord who acts in good faith incurs no liability for refusing to allow access or provide keys to the rental unit to the excluded tenant or refusing to help the excluded tenant obtain belongings in the rental.

If the provider of the utilities, such as the electric company, shuts off your service because you haven't paid bills that are your responsibility, you won't have any rights against the landlord unless a habitability violation caused your bills to be unusually high. Sometimes a defective electric water heater causes an abnormally high consumption of electricity; a running toilet will greatly inflate your water bill. If the landlord is responsible, it may take a court order to deal with the problem. If it's your fault (or if a court order is taking too long), you may be able to convince the utility company to restore service by making some kind of payment arrangement. If the utility is covered by the Oregon Public Utilities Commission (PUC), it may help negotiate with the provider.

A municipal utility — electricity, garbage, water, natural gas, or domestic water provided by a city, county, or utility district — can transfer to the landlord a claim against a tenant for unpaid utility bills, but only if the utility provided notice to the tenant and mailed a copy of the notice of delinquency by first-class mail to the last address of the owner or owner's agent within 30 days from the time the payment was due on the account. Similarly, a municipal utility can deny or shut off service to a tenant based on its lien for unpaid claims for services furnished to a previous tenant, but only if the utility notified the owner or the owner's agent of the delinquency by mailing a copy of the notice of delinquency by first-class mail to the last address of the owner or agent on file with the utility at the time the notice was sent to the tenant.

Municipal utilities that impose liens for unpaid utility services or deny services to a tenant based on nonpayment by previous tenants are subject to three requirements designed to protect the interests of landlords and tenants:

- These municipal utilities are required to deny service to a tenant who owes a previous bill to the utility unless the municipal utility and the tenant agree to a repayment plan.

- Whatever policy these municipal utilities maintain for single-family-dwelling nonpayment shutoffs must be the same for owner-occupied and tenant-occupied residences.

- These municipal utilities are required to provide information about the status of a tenant's account to the landlord, and have no liability for disclosure to a person who is not an owner or agent of an owner.

To reduce water service shutoffs by municipal utilities when water bills are not paid, ORS 223.594 provides that when water service is provided to a multifamily building with five or more units on a single water meter (or to several parcels of property under a single owner and served by the same water meter), the owner is considered the user of the water. If payment is not made when due and the water "has not been shut off or will not be shut off," the municipal utility may place a lien on the real property for the amount of the unpaid water bill.

2. Abuse of Access

Landlords' and tenants' rights concerning inspections of the premises and other landlord entries are discussed in chapter 1. This section lists the remedies available to a tenant whose landlord violates the right of privacy by making unlawful entries, lawful entries in an unreasonable manner, or repeated demands for entries that are otherwise lawful but have the effect of unreasonably harassing the tenant (ORS 90.322). The remedies include —

- a court order restraining the landlord from making such entries or demands,

- terminating the rental agreement if the tenant chooses, and

- actual damages (which can include emotional distress) of at least one month's rent.

Again, see an attorney if you can't work out a solution.

ORLTA authorizes the landlord to have a key to the rental. As a practical matter, the landlord may need to get into the tenant's home in a real emergency while the tenant is gone. Under some circumstances, the tenant could be held responsible for the cost of repairing damage done to get in without a key. Still, a tenant should be able to install a chain lock to increase security while at home. For more effective exclusion of an abusive landlord, the tenant will likely need a court order.

3. Wrongful Seizure of Personal Belongings

A landlord may not seize a tenant's belongings to enforce a claim for unpaid rent (ORS 90.420). A landlord who wrongfully seizes and retains property to enforce a rent claim is in double trouble: not only is the tenant entitled to recover up to twice the actual damages, but the tenant is also relieved of any responsibility for any rent that was owing at the time of the seizure (ORS 90.425).

Once a landlord understands that there is no lawful basis for holding onto a tenant's seized belongings to extract payment for unpaid rent or damages, he or she may back down. It is a drastic mistake for a landlord to try to coerce a settlement in return for release of the goods. Doing so would only increase the tenant's chances of winning damages in court, and a release of claims by the tenant given just to stop a clearly illegal seizure won't hold up in court.

A landlord who returns the goods may want a signed receipt from the tenant, who should not sign unless he or she is sure that everything has come back in satisfactory condition.

CHAPTER EIGHT

EVICTIONS AND DEFENSES

If a landlord wants a residential tenant to move out for a lawful reason, the landlord need only follow three steps:

(a) Give the tenant appropriate written notice

(b) File an eviction case if the tenant is still in the rental after the notice period ends

(c) Arrange for a sheriff to enforce the court's judgment of restitution if the tenant does not move out after the court judgment

In the vast majority of cases, the process is just that simple. This chapter will outline the process to help landlords keep it that way, by choosing the appropriate kind of eviction. It will describe to landlords and tenants alike the kinds of defenses and counterclaims tenants can raise in each kind of case. For both sides, this chapter should provide some guidelines as to whether the problem between the parties is really worth fighting over. See the Appendix for the flowchart process of residential eviction. The flowchart also includes the corresponding ORS numbers for the different procedures.

Oregon landlords cannot use "self-help" to evict tenants. Trying to throw out a tenant without proper notice or without using the full court process can result in a judgment for significant damages to a wrongfully ousted tenant, and, in some cases, the landlord being charged with a crime. There is only one very narrow exception to this rule: at the request and only at the request of a tenant who is the victim of domestic violence, stalking, or sexual assault by a co-tenant, the landlord can change locks and otherwise keep the co-tenant out of the victim's rental. (See lockouts, chapter 7.) The landlord does not even have to give the co-tenant notice of this change.

The landlord who wins an eviction case is entitled to recover court costs from the evicted tenant, but can be awarded attorney fees payable by the tenant only if the tenant contests the case (ORS 105.137). Therefore, a tenant with little likelihood of success in court will need to decide whether the cost to file an answer is worth it when a loss can mean not only homelessness but also debt. At the same time, some courts sponsor landlord-tenant mediation that is available only if tenants contest the case. Mediation can sometimes be the tenant's only avenue to a second chance.

What should a tenant do when faced with eviction? One option is to move away within the time period given in the notice. In such a case, the landlord should not have to file a case, so there will be no additional costs and no public record of the termination of the tenancy. The tenant who does not move but does nothing else either will be evicted; the landlord automatically wins when the tenant does not file an answer (a legal form that contains defenses against the landlord's claims). After the landlord gets a judgment of restitution and contacts the sheriff to remove the tenant, the tenant will get a final notice from the sheriff giving him or her only four days in which to leave or be removed from the property (ORS 105.151). The tenant who fights an eviction and wins gets to keep living in his or her current home, is awarded court costs and attorney fees if represented, and may get a judgment for money damages from the landlord.

1. Starting an Eviction Case — Proper Notice and Filing

An eviction case does not begin when the landlord files a complaint at the courthouse, but instead begins with the notice the landlord gives the tenant announcing the intent to terminate the rental agreement. In every situation except one (not counting the domestic-violence co-tenant situation mentioned above), the landlord must give proper notice before filing a court case.

The exception is when a tenancy has expired by its own terms (ORS 90.100(15); ORS 105.115(2)). A typical example is when a one-year lease has come to an end, and the agreement does not allow for automatic renewal or contain language that would convert the tenancy to some other kind of relationship. A landlord who accepts rent for a period after the lease ends starts a new month-to-month tenancy; a landlord who files eviction papers does not. (It is hard to imagine why a landlord would want to pay court filing fees rather than give the tenant some kind of notice beforehand that doesn't cost the landlord anything, but the law allows for it.)

In all other situations, the landlord must give written notice. There are two basic categories of notice — "for cause" (caused by the tenant's conduct) and "no cause" (there is always some reason, but this means not the result of the tenant's conduct). For the landlord who can give a lawful no-cause notice, the minimum amount of notice is 30 days in a month-to-month agreement — with one exception — and 10 days in a week-to-week agreement (ORS 90.427). The exception is a tenancy for rented space not in a facility when the tenant owns the manufactured dwelling or floating home. In that situation, the no-cause notice must give no fewer than 180 days (ORS 90.429).

The notice in these situations must state the amount of time and designate the termination date itself. In counting the days, the landlord cannot count the day the notice is given as the first day; the next day is the first day. The designated termination date does not end until midnight — after the courthouse is closed. (In the case of 24-hour notices based on dangerous or outrageous behavior, the midnight deadline does not apply. The landlord can use an actual hour.) When the notice is mailed, the designated termination date must be at least three days later to accommodate the extra mail time, except in the mobile or floating home exception above (ORS 90.155; ORS 90.160). A hand-written notice is fine, so long as it has the necessary information. See Samples 14 and 15. In most cases, the landlord can use a preprinted standard notice form, though it is important to know which is the right form. (If you are paying a lawyer to draft a single-spaced four-page notice of termination, you are probably paying for much more than you need.) The landlord must make a copy of the notice to attach to a court complaint for eviction, and the complaint cannot be filed until the notice period is over.

SAMPLE 14
NO-CAUSE EVICTION NOTICE

March 1, 20--

I. M. Tenant
#107–123 Tenant Lane
Portland, Oregon

To I.M. Tenant:

I hereby give you notice that your tenancy at #107–23 Tenant Lane, Portland, Oregon, will terminate on April 1, 20-- *[date at least 30 days later, or at least 33 days later if notice mailed]*.

Myra Smith
(Landlord) Myra Smith

While it is important for a landlord to have legal advice before seeking to evict a tenant, the landlord does not usually need a lawyer to draft the court complaint. The court clerk's office provides a form for this purpose. The landlord, an agent for the landlord, or the landlord's attorney can sign the complaint form (ORS 105.130). The form is designed for the "fast track" eviction process, however, so it does not include a claim for back rent or damages. The landlord who wants to sue for all of these things at once will have to use a different, slower process that will be best undertaken by a lawyer (Oregon Rule of Civil Procedure [ORCP] 24).

To start a plain eviction case, the landlord must pay the court clerk the necessary fees at the time of filing. The clerk can quote the current cost. The court clerk then arranges to have a copy of the complaint mailed to the tenant and another formally served on the tenant. The complaint will state the date by which the tenant must "answer" by showing up for a "first appearance," usually set for seven days after the day the landlord pays the complaint

SAMPLE 15
NOTICE OF EVICTION FOR CAUSE

March 1, 20--

I. M. Tenant
#107–123 Tenant Lane
Portland, Oregon

To I.M. Tenant:

You have breached clause 22a of your rental agreement by removing a portion of the hedge that separates your yard from the yard of the tenant in unit #108. This damage is a material breach of your rental agreement. For that reason, your tenancy will terminate as of April 1, 20-- *[date at least 30 days later, or at least 33 days later if notice mailed]*.

You can avoid termination by replacing the hedge with the same kind and size of hedge as that you removed, and by replacing it no later than March 15, 20-- *[date at least 14 days later, or at least 17 days later if notice mailed]*.

Myra Smith
(Landlord) Myra Smith

filing fees. The sheriff or a civil process server or any legally competent person age 18 or older (and not involved in the case in any way) can perform the formal service. To do this, the server must hand the papers to the tenant or, if the tenant cannot be found, attach the papers securely to the main entrance of the rental (ORS 105.135). In an apartment building, the papers would go on the door to the tenant's apartment, not on the main door of the building. The server must then complete a "certificate of service" and submit it immediately to the court clerk (ORCP 7).

At the first appearance, several things can happen. If the landlord shows up and the tenant doesn't, the landlord will win automatically, getting a judgment of restitution and an order for court costs. If the tenant appears and the landlord does not, the tenant wins automatically (ORS 105.137). If neither party appears, the court should dismiss the landlord's case. If the landlord shows up and the tenant wants to contest the eviction, the tenant will have to file a form answer or an answer with counterclaims (there is no form for this purpose) by the end of the business day. The trial must then be set no later than 15 days after the first appearance. A tenant who has no legal defense or who does not want to have a trial can show up at the first appearance for the sole purpose of asking the judge for a few extra days to move out. What can happen at trial will depend on the defenses and counterclaims the tenant raises, which are discussed later in this chapter.

The landlord can postpone the trial simply by asking for a continuance (in some counties this must be done in writing); the tenant, on the other hand, may be ordered to pay rent as it accrues into court if the trial must be delayed for any reason other than at the landlord's request and if, after a hearing, the court concludes that requiring the tenant to pay rent into court is "just and equitable." A tenant who can show (through documents, photographs, or testimony) that he or she has strong claims against the landlord for reduced rent or damages should be able to convince the judge that payment would not be appropriate during a brief delay.

2. For-Cause and No-Cause Evictions

Many landlords say that they never use "for cause" termination notices, and that this kind of notice should be avoided. This landlord fear is misplaced. In practice, it is a for-cause notice (for non-payment of rent) that is the most commonly used notice underlying eviction cases. Over-reliance on no-cause notices can cause just as many problems for landlords.

There are legitimate reasons to give "no cause" notices, such as when the landlord is selling the property, the landlord wants to move into the property, the landlord's relative wants to move into the property, the landlord is planning to raise the rent for a lawful reason beyond the level the current tenant can pay, or the landlord wants to remodel the property. However, some landlords mistakenly believe that they can give no-cause notices "for any reason or no reason," which is not true.

There are limits on no-cause evictions, such as —

- they are not available before the end of a fixed-term tenancy or lease,

- they are not available in some kinds of federally funded housing or subsidized rent situations,

- they may not be available in manufactured dwelling facilities for tenants who rent only space, and

- they are not a very good alternative to exercising responsible business judgment.

Example: A landlord who is annoyed with a particular tenant may want to succumb to a knee-jerk reaction to evict for "no cause." A knee-jerk reaction to a tenant can cost the landlord money if the underlying reason happens to be illegal. The tenant may be able to respond with a defense to the eviction; for instance, unlawful retaliation, unlawful discrimination, or unlawful debt collection. The landlord may wind up paying damages and attorney fees, and still have the tenant. Even if the tenant doesn't resist eviction, the landlord now must spend time and money finding a new tenant who is likely to be an "unknown quantity." The smart landlord will pause to weigh the business ramifications and alternatives before evicting for "no cause" that is actually based on personal dislike or mere ego conflict.

In most cases when the tenant's conduct is the problem confronting the landlord, getting the tenant to change behavior is preferable from a business standpoint to changing to a new tenant. In nonemergency situations under a month-to-month rental agreement or fixed-term lease, a minimum 30-day for-cause termination notice gives the landlord the leverage to encourage new behavior without sacrificing the right to evict if the tenant doesn't want to make a reasonable change. The key is "reasonable," of course. Nonemergency for-cause notice works when —

there is material noncompliance by the tenant with the rental agreement, a noncompliance with basic tenant day-to-day maintenance materially affecting health and safety, a material noncompliance with a rental agreement regarding a program of recovery in drug- and alcohol-free housing or a failure to pay a late charge … (ORS 90.400(1)).

In week-to-week tenancies, the notice period is seven days. This kind of notice would be appropriate for the tenant who has rowdy parties, plays the stereo so loudly that the people across the hall can't sleep, doesn't take out the trash when it is clearly past time to do so. This notice can also apply to situations where the tenant refuses to give a landlord reasonable access to the rental for inspections or repairs (ORS 90.322). This kind of notice must describe the offending conduct and give the tenant 14 days to "cure" — end the conduct — under a month-to-month rental agreement. In a week-to-week agreement, the notice must give the offending tenant four days to end the conduct. If the conduct does not change within the "fix it" period, the landlord has the right to begin eviction proceedings after the termination date on the notice. In cases when the tenant's conduct is dangerous or outrageous, for-cause notice can be very short and does not have to give the tenant the option to change behavior.

If, after receiving the for-cause notice, the tenant does not stop the offending conduct within the required time period, the landlord can proceed to court as described above. If the tenant does stop the conduct within the allotted time, the landlord may not proceed — and has no reason to.

Sometimes the change in behavior doesn't last. If, within six months of the issuance of this kind of notice, a tenant repeats the conduct that was the basis for the first notice, the landlord can issue a 10-day for-cause notice without an opportunity to change conduct the second time. In a week-to-week tenancy the period is four days. (The 10-day no-choice notice cannot be used in a case based on nonpayment of rent for the current month.) In a manufactured dwelling facility, the rules are different. (See chapter 13.) A landlord who is basing an eviction on a second for-cause notice of this type should append both the first and the second notices to the eviction complaint to show he or she has complied with all of the steps in the process.

2.1 Evictions for nonpayment of rent

The most common for-cause notice is for nonpayment of rent. The landlord can use a 30-day (seven days in week-to-week tenancies) for-cause notice for this purpose, or a faster notice specifically for nonpayment of rent. If the tenant then pays the rent by mail, rent is considered paid on the date sent. If the landlord wants late rent payments not to be mailed, the rental agreement itself and the notice of nonpayment must allow the tenant to pay at the rental or at the location where the tenant has made all prior in-person rent payments. That location must be available for payment throughout the notice period. Furthermore, the nonpayment notice must be either personally delivered to the tenant or mailed and attached to the tenant's entryway (ORS 90.400).

For month-to-month tenancies, the nonpayment notice can be a 72-hour notice delivered on or after the 8th day of the rental period or a 144-hour notice delivered on or after the 5th day of the rental period. (See Sample 16.) Either way, the landlord who delivers this kind of notice as soon as it is lawful to do so must wait until at least the 11th day of the rental period, and until the end of the notice period in any case, before starting a case in court. Mailed notices must give the tenant three additional days to comply. In a week-to-week tenancy, the landlord can give only a 72-hour notice, but can give the notice on day five of the rental period.

SAMPLE 16
NOTICE OF TERMINATION FOR NONPAYMENT OF RENT (72-HOUR NOTICE)

March 8, 20--

I. M. Tenant
123 Tenant Lane
Portland, Oregon

To Ms. I. M. Tenant:

Your rent for 123 Tenant Lane, in the amount of $615, was due as of March 1, 20--, but has not yet been paid. Unless you pay the rent by midnight March 11, 20--, I will terminate our rental agreement and begin an eviction case.

Myra Smith
(Landlord) Myra Smith

If the tenant tenders the overdue rent within the required time period, the landlord may not refuse it, even if the tenant owes late charges. The landlord cannot then proceed with an eviction based on nonpayment of rent. However, the landlord can use a 30-day for-cause notice to force payment of any remaining late fees or charges, or a 30-day no-cause notice to end the tenancy altogether for lawful reasons. A court might question the good faith of a landlord who gives one notice ostensibly offering the tenant the option to stay while at the same time giving the tenant a notice that offers no opportunity to stay.

2.2 Evictions for pet violations

The landlord can force a tenant to decide between moving out and getting rid of an unpermitted pet "capable of causing damage to persons or property" with a minimum 10 days' notice citing the reason and designating the final day to comply to avoid eviction (see Sample 17). Note that a medium or large fish tank meets the requirement of this section of the law (ORS 90.405). The landlord can give a no-choice notice giving the reason and 10 days for the tenant to move out if the tenant repeats the offense within six months of the issuance of the first notice. The landlord should attach both notices to the eviction complaint to show compliance with all the steps in the notice process. The law is different for tenants who rent space in manufactured housing facilities. (See chapter 13.)

2.3 Evictions from drug-free and alcohol-free housing

There are four situations that involve short-notice procedures and all of them involve serious problems. The first short-notice situation applies to drug-and-alcohol-free housing, as defined in ORS 90.243. Only landlords who are housing authorities or nonprofit organizations can use this kind of notice, and even they can use this kind of notice only for certain kinds of rentals:

- At least four contiguous units in a complex with fewer than nine rentals are each used exclusively for occupancies by at least one person in a recovery program for alcohol or drug addiction, or at least eight contiguous units are such in a complex with more than nine units, or, if there are fewer than four units in a complex designated as drug- and alcohol-free housing, that each unit that becomes available is then designated drug- and alcohol-free.

SAMPLE 17
NOTICE OF TERMINATION FOR PET VIOLATION

March 1, 20--

I. M. Tenant
123 Tenant Lane
Portland, Oregon

To Ms. I. M. Tenant:

Although your rental agreement specifies that you may not keep a dog at your rental, you are now keeping a dog there. Unless you remove the dog no later than March 11, 20-- *[date at least 10 days after date of notice, or 13 days if notice mailed]*, your tenancy will terminate on April 1, 20-- *[date at least 30 days after date of notice, or 33 days if notice mailed]*.

Myra Smith
(Landlord) Myra Smith

- The designated units are drug and alcohol free not only for tenants but for staff and guests.

- Tenants may neither possess nor use, nor permit others to possess or use, alcohol or illegal or unauthorized drugs.

- Tenants participate in recovery programs that verify non-use.

- There is a written rental agreement that allows monitoring for compliance and gives the landlord the right to terminate the tenancy for noncompliance with alcohol-free and drug-free rules.

- The written rental agreement states that the failure of a tenant to take a test for drug or alcohol usage is considered evidence of use.

In the case of a drug or alcohol violation by a tenant who has lived less than two years in drug- and alcohol-free housing, the landlord can give a minimum of a 48-hour for-cause notice to the tenant. The notice must give the tenant 24 hours to cure the violation (by stopping use) to avoid eviction. A second violation within six months gives the landlord the right to evict after 24 hours for-cause notice.

2.4 Evictions of illegal subtenants

A 24-hour notice of termination can be issued against an illegal subtenant — someone who moved in with the consent of a former tenant that moved out and sublet or assigned the rental to the new person in violation of a written rental agreement. Before a landlord can use this type of notice, the real tenant must have already vacated the rental, the rental agreement between that person and the landlord must have prohibited subleasing or other occupants without written permission of the landlord, and the landlord must not knowingly have accepted rent from the new occupant. (See Sample 18.)

2.5 Evictions for personal injury, property damage, and outrageous conduct

The final two situations involve conduct by a tenant or a tenant's guest or a tenant's pet that is violent, imminently violent, outrageous, or — in the case of humans — criminal. ORS 90.400(2) permits a landlord to start an eviction after 24 hours' written notice stating the cause but not giving the tenant a chance to stop the violation in these circumstances. The landlord may serve such a notice if the tenant or someone in the tenant's control —

- seriously threatens substantial harm or actually inflicts substantial harm on anyone other than the tenant, on or in the immediate vicinity of the premises (this includes the tenant's pet causing harm to someone other than the tenant);

- recklessly endangers someone other than the tenant on the premises by creating a serious risk of substantial harm;

- substantially damages the premises even one time, or permits the tenant's pet to do so more than one time (see Sample 19);

- sublets to someone the premises in violation of a sublease prohibition or without permission of the landlord, from whom the landlord has not knowingly accepted rent; or

SAMPLE 18
NOTICE OF EVICTION FOR PROHIBITED SUBTENANCY

March 1, 20--

I. M. Tenant
123 Tenant Lane
Portland, Oregon

To Ms. I. M. Tenant:

My former tenant at 123 Tenant Lane, Portland, Oregon, signed a lease that expressly prohibited subletting, assigning, or allowing another person to occupy that rental without my written permission. It is my understanding that the tenant has moved out, but no one asked my permission for you to move in. It is my practice to screen applicants before renting to them, and I have not accepted you as a tenant.

I hereby give you notice that if you are not out of the rental within 24 hours of your receipt of this notice *[or 24 hours from the time of mailing and attaching the notice to tenant's entryway]*, I will start an eviction case to have you removed.

You may apply to rent the place right away, but unless and until I accept you as a tenant, I do not consent to your being in the unit.

Myra Smith
(Landlord) Myra Smith

- commits any act that is "outrageous in the extreme," such as drug manufacturing (but not minor marijuana offenses and the use of medical marijuana), prostitution, gambling, intimidation, burglary, etc. Although the conduct does not, technically, need to be a crime to meet the standard of outrageous in the extreme, a court will expect the conduct complained of to be highly offensive if the conduct is not in fact serious and imminently dangerous.

The landlord can also serve notice if the tenant lied on the rental application received by the landlord in the last year about criminal convictions that would have made the landlord reject the tenancy, and the landlord gives notice within 30 days of finding out the truth.

The landlord can choose to give a 48-hour notice about a destructive or dangerous pet, with 24 hours for the tenant to remove

SAMPLE 19
NOTICE OF EVICTION FOR SUBSTANTIAL DAMAGE

March 1, 20--

I. M. Tenant
123 Tenant Lane
Portland, Oregon

To Ms. I. M. Tenant:

Last night you intentionally inflicted substantial damage to your apartment by knocking down a wall with a sledgehammer. For that reason, your rental agreement will be terminated 24 hours from your receipt of this notice *[or 24 hours from the time of mailing and attaching the notice to tenant's entryway]*. If you have not moved out by then, I will start an eviction case against you.

Myra Smith

(Landlord) Myra Smith

the pet permanently. If the pet returns, the landlord can give a 24-hour eviction notice with no opportunity to cure so long as the notice cites the earlier notice. **Note:** Both notices should accompany the landlord's court complaint.

A landlord who wants to terminate an employee who is living in one of the landlord's rentals may have some difficulty choosing the proper notice if he or she also wants the employee to move out. (See the section on tenant's defenses, below.) Generally speaking, an employee who is brought into the premises for the sole purpose of performing the job (such as residence managing) can be evicted through the usual court process after a 24-hour termination of employment notice. (For the employer who provides housing for farm worker employees, however, federal and state employment law dictate whether and when the landlord can lawfully fire and evict. A violation of labor law can have much greater penalties than a violation of ORLTA.) An employee who is already a tenant when hired cannot be evicted on such a notice, and has the protections that other tenants have.

Once the notice period for each kind of notice has ended, the landlord may proceed as with any other eviction case, described above. In any of these situations, the landlord must attach to the court complaint a copy of the notice relied on for the eviction (ORS 105.124). That requirement means that landlords must keep and copy for-cause notices that preceded a final for-cause notice with no opportunity to cure. Landlords faced with dangerous or seriously destructive tenants should see chapter 9.

3. Tenant Defenses Against Attempts to Evict Them

Tenant defenses vary according to the kind of —

- rental agreement tenants have (verbal or written, week-to-week, month-to-month, or lease);

- housing they live in (their own manufactured home or rented space, drug- and alcohol-free housing, private landlord rental, government subsidized), and

- notice they have received (for-cause, no-cause, or no notice at all).

Table 2 shows the kinds of evictions possible and the defenses available to tenants in most kinds of housing. See also chapter 12 (government-financed or subsidized housing) and chapter 13 (manufactured dwelling facilities). This section discusses eviction defenses in general, so that both landlords and tenants can understand how a court will look at them.

3.1 The retaliatory eviction defense

A landlord may have refused to renew a lease or accept rent that would begin a new month-to-month tenancy in order to retaliate against a tenant. A landlord may have served an unlawful no-cause notice, or a nonpayment-of-rent notice in retaliation for a tenant's lawful withholding of rent (ORS 90.385) (manufactured and floating home facilities as well; ORS 90.765). ORLTA prohibits a landlord from increasing rent, decreasing services, serving a notice of termination, or starting or threatening to start an eviction after the tenant has —

(a) complained verbally or in writing to a government agency about a building, health or safety code violation materially affecting health or safety; laws or regulations about the delivery of mail; or laws or regulations prohibiting discrimination in rental housing;

(b) notified the landlord in writing of the tenant's intent to complain to an agency about such a violation;

(c) complained, verbally or in writing, to the landlord in good faith about anything relating to the tenancy;

(d) organized or joined a tenants' union;

(e) testified against the landlord in any judicial, administrative, or legislative proceeding;

(f) successfully defended against an eviction attempt by this landlord within the last six months for reasons other than those about defects of notices or the service of those notices; or

(g) performed or expressed the intent to perform any other act for the purpose of asserting, protecting or invoking the protection of any tenant right under any law. (For example, a tenant may insist on receiving a receipt as a condition of paying rent, a right under ORS 90.140.)

TABLE 2
EVICTIONS AND DEFENSES

DEFENSES AVAILABLE	No notice	No cause	For cause	Nonpayment of rent	Substantial injury	Pet violation	Illegal subtenant	Resident manager	Drug/alcohol
Unlawful discrimination	X	X	X				X		
Retaliation	X	X	X	X	X	X	X		X
Equity	X	X	X	X	X	X	X	X	
Terms of the rental agreement	X	X	X	X	X	X	X		X
Waiver or new tenancy	X	X	X	X	X	X	X	X	X
Prepaid rent period	X		X	X					
Defective notice		X	X	X	X	X	X	X	X
Breach did not occur or was not material			X		X	X			X
Breach cured or offered cure refused			X	X		X			X
Breach was of void term or rule			X			X			
Rent not due or subject to recoupment or counterclaim				X					
Rent offered but rejected				X					
Injury not substantial or threat not serious					X				
Wrong kind of tenancy	X	X						X	X
Access was not unlawfully refused	X								
Defective service of notice		X	X	X	X	X	X		X
Mobile home tenancy	X	X				X			
Pet incapable of damage						X			
No written rental agreement								X	X
Original tenant still there							X		
Occupancy not conditioned on employment	X							X	

The retaliation defense will work only if the tenant can convince the court that, but for the tenant's exercise of one or more of the rights listed above, the landlord would not have started the eviction case. It is up to the tenant to present evidence — facts — that the eviction is retaliatory. Generally this is done by showing a sequence of events, such as that the landlord gave an eviction notice or a notice of rent increase soon after the tenant asked for repairs or told the landlord about a rent withhold.

Retaliation is not available as a defense to a tenant who is behind in rent; but a tenant who has withheld rent, as described in chapter 6, is not considered behind in rent. A tenant cannot say a landlord is retaliating if the tenant's complaint to or about the landlord was about a condition that is the tenant's fault.

Finally, a landlord could convince the court that, even though there are serious habitability problems with the rental, they are so serious the tenant has to move out permanently. The courts have interpreted this part of the statute to mean that a government agency is forcing the landlord to remove the tenant. If the agency isn't in court to say that, the tenant will need to point out that the landlord hasn't proved this part of the case. The tenant may even want to subpoena a witness from an agency that has inspected the place, if that person can say the place could be repaired without making it impossible for the tenant to live there.

The retaliation defense can be fairly difficult to present; having legal counsel can be extremely important.

3.2 The discrimination defense

Under ORS 90.390, discrimination can be a defense to an eviction if the tenant can prove that the real motive for the eviction was to discriminate against the tenant for one of the reasons prohibited. (See chapter 14 for a description of different kinds of discrimination.) Some examples of discrimination are as follows: the tenant adopted a baby or became pregnant; the tenant's new wife or girlfriend is Catholic, or Iranian, or Jewish, or Nigerian, or Peruvian, etc.; or a tenant with a disability asked for permission to install ramps for access, or obtained an assistance animal.

The landlord-tenant statute doesn't allow the use of the discrimination defense if the tenant is behind in rent. However, a tenant who has a strong claim of discrimination and who acts fast to get legal counsel may be able to get his or her eviction case stopped while a fair housing agency investigates and perhaps even tries to resolve the discrimination issue. That resolution could easily include a stop to the attempt to evict.

3.3 Equitable defense

The courts that handle eviction cases have two kinds of power: they can award damages for past harm, and they can force the parties to do or refrain from doing certain things in the future (e.g., forcing tenants to move out or forcing landlords to make repairs or turn on utilities that have been shut off illegally). This second kind of power is part of the court's "equity" power — the power to achieve a fair outcome.

Equity should work as a defense in this common example of landlord bad faith: Landlord intentionally leads tenant to believe that a month-to-month tenancy will be long-term, and encourages the tenant to paint the house, landscape the yard, and plant a garden. As soon as the tenant finishes these things, the landlord serves a termination notice. A tenant who can show that the landlord's plan was to get free labor from the tenant should prevail in an eviction action. (ORLTA spells out that the parties must act in good faith before they have the right to use the law to enforce their rights [ORS 90.130].)

To many tenants, it may not seem fair for a landlord to be able to evict a tenant who has lost a job and cannot pay rent, or someone who has a new baby but no income. Extreme hardship alone is not enough to enable a tenant to win an eviction case. In many cases, however, judges have briefly postponed the enforcement of an eviction judgment — a few days to two weeks — to reduce hardship to a low-income family about to become homeless.

3.4 Federal housing rights

If the tenancy somehow involves one of the several federally financed programs that assist landlords in providing rental housing or that assist tenants in paying for housing, federal law may provide the tenant with defenses that would otherwise be unavailable. Federal housing law is both complicated and rapidly changing; see chapters 12 and 15 for more information. Again, access to legal advice early can make a big difference. Legal aid offices generally have the most experience with federal housing eviction defenses. They also generally make a point of trying to serve those living in, or trying to move into, federally subsidized housing; tenants who call a legal aid office for help should be sure to alert the staff if they have a rent subsidy or live in a federally-funded complex.

3.5 Terms in the rental agreement

The landlord may file a complaint based on no notice, claiming the rental agreement expired by its own terms. If there is no written rental agreement, there can be no automatic expiration. If there is a written rental agreement that does not expressly dispense with the notice requirement, there must be notice before the landlord can start an eviction. If the landlord has accepted rent from the tenant since the alleged end of the rental agreement, then it is possible that a new tenancy has started (see waiver defense, section 10) and notice based on the new tenancy must be given.

The rental agreement may contain a provision for informal dispute resolution in general or mediation in particular before an eviction case can be started. If the landlord did not follow this step, there should be no attempt to evict unless and until that step has proved unsuccessful. If the rental agreement says that rent is due on the 15th day of the month, the landlord cannot claim the rent was overdue on the 11th day of the month. If the rental agreement is a term lease, the landlord cannot evict during the term of the lease for "no cause." Instead the landlord must give the proper good-cause notice and, if that kind of notice provides for it, give the tenant the opportunity to correct the problem.

3.6 Prepaid rent defense

A tenant who has paid for rent into the future has a defense against a no-cause termination notice (ORS 105.120). The landlord must wait to file a case "until after the expiration of any period for which the tenant ... has paid the rent in advance." There are two exceptions to this defense. The first one is that the tenant cannot claim the "last month's rent" deposit as rent paid in advance. The second exception arises if the landlord has given a valid notice to terminate, the tenant has paid rent for a period beyond the termination date in the notice, and the landlord has refunded the unused portion of the rent (that is, any portion that would cover a period past the termination date) within six days of receiving it.

3.7 Defenses to specific kinds of for-cause evictions

All of the defenses listed above for no-cause eviction attempts apply to for-cause evictions as well. In addition, there are defenses specific to the kind of cause the landlord alleges.

3.7a No opportunity to "cure" violations

The most common landlord misunderstanding and misuse of for-cause evictions is that, after giving the proper notice, the landlord does not permit the tenant to correct the problem that would keep the tenancy from terminating.

> **Example:** The landlord rejects rent that is given in a timely response to a 72-hour notice, or refuses to acknowledge that a tenant has taken a prohibited pet to the humane society even when the tenant presents a receipt.

For tenants in this situation, the defense is that they "cured the breach" or that the landlord "refused the cure they offered." The tenant must present evidence that shows he or she did correct the problem the landlord complained about, and, just as important, corrected the problem within the time limit the law required. (**Note:** A notice giving the tenant 10 days to get rid of an unauthorized pet is effective to support an eviction if the tenant gets rid of the pet on day 11.)

Some landlords make up their own deadlines for compliance, far short of what the law provides; improper deadlines can also be used as a defense for tenants. (See defective notice, section 4.)

3.7b Unreasonable rules or unfair application of rules

Another possible defense is that the landlord attempted to enforce an unreasonable rule against the tenant, or the landlord tried to enforce reasonable rules unfairly against the tenant (ORS 90.245, ORS 90.262). The tenant will need to explain how the rule is unreasonable, or how the rule is applied unfairly. (The rules may be unconscionable under ORS 90.135.)

Provisions in rental agreements are unenforceable if —

- they are so harsh, one-sided, or shocking that only a desperate person would agree to such terms;

- their purpose is to waive tenants rights under ORLTA;

- they authorize the landlord to get a judgment against a tenant without an opportunity for a court hearing; or

- they are designed to protect the landlord from consequences of the landlord's willful misconduct or negligence.

A rule is unenforceable if —

- the tenant had no notice of it when the tenancy started or when the rule was adopted;

- it isn't reasonably related to its supposed purpose;

- it doesn't promote the convenience, safety, or welfare of the tenant, protect landlord property, or distribute services and facilities fairly among tenants;

- it doesn't apply fairly to all tenants;

- it's not clear and understandable; or

- it substantially changed the tenant's rights without his or her written consent.

The basis for evictions due to changes in rules in facilities for manufactured dwellings or floating homes are somewhat different; see chapter 13 for a full discussion. It is important to note that a facility rule cannot be the basis for eviction unless the rental agreement specifies that violation of that rule is a ground for termination.

4. Defective Notice

The requirements for each kind of termination notice are discussed above. In addition to specific requirements for particular situations, they all must meet these general requirements:

- The notice must be in writing.

- The notice must state the actual date of termination, and the termination date must be at least as many days away as the law requires for that notice type (ORS 90.400, ORS 90.427, ORS 90.429, ORS 90.630, ORS 90.632).

- The notice must be signed by the landlord or an authorized agent.

- If served by mail only, the notice must extend the termination date by three days (see ORS 90.155).

If the notice the tenant receives does not meet these requirements, the tenant may have a defense to the eviction on this basis alone. The notice also must be clearly intended to terminate the rental agreement: "Get out or pay twice the normal rent" will not satisfy the requirement of the law. In the rare case when no termination notice is required, this defense obviously won't help the tenant.

5. Defective Service of Notice

When an eviction requires some kind of notice, that notice must be served on the tenant. ORLTA allows service of notices to be done personally by the landlord or anyone the landlord designates, or by first-class mail (ORS 90.150). If mailed only, the notice must allow an additional three days for compliance (ORS 90.155). A written rental agreement can provide for landlord notices to be attached to the entry to the tenant's home so long as copies are mailed at the same time. In that case, there is no three-day addition to the notice period. A landlord may not use certified mail to give termination notices; often certified mail is left unclaimed. The law presumes that a letter with the proper address, postage, and return address is received.

Sometimes a tenant will be able to prove that the notice was not received, or not received timely, if mailed. (Yes, there actually are a few scurrilous landlords who will send the notice, then steal it out of the tenant's mailbox when it arrives at the tenant's home!) The tenant should check the postmark on the envelope, and keep the envelope for use in court if the cancellation mark is so late that the tenant did not receive the amount of notice required.

6. Material Noncompliance

One of the reasons a landlord can use a for-cause termination is a material noncompliance with the rental agreement, or a noncompliance with the tenant's basic duty to care properly for the rental that materially affects health and safety. A material noncompliance is one that is rationally important to the landlord, not one that is just technical, minor, or unimportant. For example, messy housekeeping is noncompliant if it damages the landlord's property, creates a fire hazard, or attracts rats and cockroaches.

How can a tenant show that a noncompliance isn't material? He or she can ask a fire inspector or building inspector to look at the place. There should be no issue about fire hazards so long as hot surfaces like heaters aren't too close to the tenant's belongings or anything else that might be flammable, and there are clear paths to exit doors and windows. The tenant may be able to convince the landlord not to go forward on this kind of notice by giving the landlord a copy of the inspector's report. If the landlord pursues the case, the tenant will have to subpoena the inspector for the trial. Even if there is no fire hazard, tenants should know that mountains of dirty dishes, trash that never gets taken outside, and piles of rotting food can provide the landlord with persuasive evidence of a health threat.

Some landlords insist that "the loud dance party on the night of October 20" simply can't be cured. The tenant can point out that the statute accepts a change of conduct as a cure. The end of the party cures the problem. If it could not be cured, loud parties would be one of the statutory examples of "outrageous in the extreme" conduct that merit a 24-hour notice. They aren't. A 30-day for-cause notice must always give the tenant the opportunity to correct a problem that can be solved "by repairs, payment of damages, payment of a late charge or utility or service charge, change in conduct or otherwise."

Another defense to a for-cause eviction is that the conduct complained of did not happen. Although the law requires the landlord to convince the judge that more likely than not the conduct did happen, quite a few judges expect the tenant to prove that the conduct didn't happen. This is hard to do; having witnesses makes it easier, of course. This issue most frequently comes up in 24-hour eviction cases. Sometimes this kind of eviction is simply a pretext for the landlord to retaliate against a tenant for exercising rights.

7. Denial of Access

A tenant can defend against a case based on a for-cause termination notice after the tenant's refusal to allow the landlord to enter the tenant's home by showing that —

- the landlord did not give advance notice before seeking entry,

- the landlord entered without notice when there was no emergency to justify it, or

- an otherwise reasonable entry was made in an unreasonable way or in a way that had the effect of harassing the tenant.

> **Example 1:** A tenant admits the landlord into the kitchen to repair the stove only to discover the landlord in the bathroom when she steps out of the shower.

> **Example 2:** A landlord with the right in the written rental agreement to care for the yard at the tenant's home starts his power mower every Sunday at 7 a.m. next to the tenant's bedroom window, despite tenant complaints about inconvenience and disturbance.

The tenant must remember that a written request for repairs that does not designate times for entry gives the landlord free reasonable entry for up to seven consecutive days — even longer if a repair is actively underway. Even in this situation, though, the tenant may be able to convince the court that the entry is unreasonable, or that repairs are not actively underway.

8. Unauthorized Pet

A tenant with an unauthorized pet must be ready to prove that the pet was removed from the property within the time allowed in the notice (minimum of ten days). A timely receipt from a humane society is helpful, as is testimony from the person who took the pet. Once in a while a landlord will give a 10-day pet violation notice because of a single goldfish in a small bowl, or a two-ounce turtle in a small terrarium. The tenant should argue that these pets and their habitat are not capable of causing harm to people or property. In some cases, a landlord's insistence on the removal of a pet may give rise to housing discrimination defenses (e.g., medically prescribed companion animals, assistance animals).

The limitations a landlord can impose on a tenant homeowner who rents space in a facility are somewhat different. For example, if a facility decides to prohibit pets and an existing tenant already has an authorized pet (including one that started out as unauthorized but became authorized as a result of the landlord's waiver), the tenant simply needs to establish that the pet was already on site and that the pet was authorized at the time that the no-pet rule went into effect. Such a tenant also can replace that pet with a similar pet without being evicted. On the other hand, the tenant would not have a defense to an eviction based on the tenant's failure to adhere to new rules about pet conduct or a requirement that the owner maintain a reasonable amount of liability insurance for the pet.

9. Nonpayment of Rent and Habitability Problems

Some unscrupulous landlords — and a few who keep very bad records — will claim that a tenant has not paid rent when in fact the tenant did pay. A tenant who can produce a receipt or a canceled check, the testimony of a witness to the payment, or evidence that the landlord was paid in kind (such as through work done by the tenant), will prevail in this kind of case. So should a tenant who insisted on getting a written receipt acknowledging the payment, and then held on to the rent money when the landlord refused to give one (ORS 90.140).

Some rental agreements allow for the payment of rent in installments (ORS 90.415). A tenant who can show the current installment has been paid on time can prevail against a nonpayment-of-rent claim in court. In cases in which there is no written rental agreement, the tenant can still prevail if he or she has receipts — or other evidence — showing regular installment payments on the same dates over a period of time (see the waiver defense, section 10).

The best way to deal with a legitimate nonpayment-of-rent notice is to pay the rent that is due within the designated period. Not having enough money to pay is not a defense. Nor is having made partial payment (for exceptions to this rule, see waiver defense, section 10).

However, when the landlord owes the tenant money at the same time because of the landlord's violations of the rental agreement or ORLTA, it may not matter whether the tenant can pay. The first question the judge should ask is not "Did the tenant pay?" but "Does the tenant owe?" because not paying the rent is not the same as being behind (in default) on the rent. Any claim the tenant has for damages arising under the rental agreement or under ORLTA can be used to defend against a nonpayment of rent eviction by offsetting the rent claimed by the landlord. For example, a tenant who can show proper use of the remedy of "repair and deduct," as described in chapter 6, should win an eviction for alleged nonpayment of rent. The tenant just needs to show notice to the landlord, the landlord's failure to act, and reasonable expenses equal to or greater than the amount of rent claimed by the landlord. The same is true for the use of substitute services and substitute housing. Furthermore, the tenant may be able to show retaliation by the landlord for the tenant's having exercised a right under ORLTA. A tenant also can withhold all or a portion of the rent as an estimate of damages due to him or her for lost value from the rental.

Ultimately, it is the judge or jury's decision how much the value of the rental home was diminished as a result of habitability problems caused by the landlord's failure to maintain or repair the unit. Landlords can put on evidence through an expert about the "market value" of a unit. But market value is not a very good measure. The court of appeals has ruled that the tenant, too, can estimate the reduced value — by dollars or percentages — because only the tenant really understands and experiences the effects of the problem. For the tenant, this calculation can be somewhat difficult, but it is necessary, because the court cannot permit a reduced value without evidence.

> **Example:** Mary looks at two apartments in the same building. One apartment has one bedroom, and rents for $450 per month; the other one has two bedrooms, and rents for $500 per month. If Mary rents the two-bedroom place and one of the bedrooms becomes unusable because of a leak in the ceiling, it is possible to say that the rental value of the apartment is reduced by $50 (the extra cost for a second bedroom). If Mary never uses the bedroom except for her mother's annual visit and she can keep the leak from damaging the place by emptying a bucket under the leak once a day, the reduction in value — to her — may be less than $50 per month. However, if Mary has two children who usually sleep and play in that room, she may be forced to put the children's beds in the living room or let the children sleep in her room — causing her loss

of sleep and privacy, and making her formerly peaceful living room noisy and cluttered with toys. This level of inconvenience may well reduce the value of the place to her by an amount much larger than $50 per month.

Another example would be a tenant living without heat in the summer in southern Oregon. It might not be an inconvenience to the tenant during the warm months in the southern region, but in the winter, in the central mountains, it would be a significant hardship.

The amount the monthly rent is reduced is multiplied by the number of months the habitability problem existed, up to one year. It is important for the tenant who claims reduced rental value to explain clearly and thoroughly how any habitability problem has changed his or her day-to-day life. If the tenant has not had to move to temporary substitute housing, however, the tenant cannot claim that the habitability defects have diminished the rental value to zero.

In a facility where the tenant rents only a space for his or her home, the tenant has a defense against a nonpayment-of-rent claim if the landlord attempts to terminate on the ground that the tenant refused to pay any one-time or periodic charge — sometimes called "pet rent" — based on the tenant's ownership of a pet. (ORS 90.530 prohibits such charges.)

10. Waiver Defense

As a general rule, a landlord can waive (lose) the right to terminate a tenancy by allowing the tenant not to comply with the rental agreement or ORLTA (ORS 90.415). The landlord does this by accepting rent over two or more rental periods knowing that the tenant is in default, or by letting the tenant behave in a way that varies from the terms of a rental agreement and then trying to terminate the agreement based on that behavior. For example, the tenant pays only a portion of the monthly rent for two months. The landlord cannot evict in the following month on a claim of nonpayment. Another example would be if a tenant gets a dog in violation of the rental agreement. The landlord sees the dog when at the rental in June, but doesn't attempt to terminate the tenancy until August based on a pet violation. In this situation, the landlord has waived the right to terminate.

"Accepting" rent has a very strict definition. Rent is accepted only if the landlord keeps it for more than six days (seven days if the tenant is a homeowner who rents space in a facility) after the tenant has paid it. If the landlord sends back the money, whether or not the tenant cashes the check is immaterial.

Under the general rule, a tenant can claim that his or her landlord waived any right to terminate for a particular cause. There are numerous exceptions to the rule, however. The tenant who wants to defeat an attempt to evict him or her should examine them carefully.

The following are the exceptions to the general rule:

- If the tenant breaches the rental agreement, the landlord and the tenant can agree afterward that the landlord has not waived the right to terminate based on that breach.

- The landlord does not waive the right to terminate pursuant to a 24-hour dangerous or outrageous conduct notice. (The tenant still has the right to question whether the conduct really happened or was bad enough to justify this emergency-level notice.)

- A landlord who accepts partial rent before giving a non-payment-of-rent notice does not waive the right to give a nonpayment notice for the balance if the tenant agreed to pay the rest by a certain date and then did not do so. However, to avoid waiver, the landlord must not serve the notice before the date the parties agreed on (or the date otherwise permissible for that kind of notice, whichever is later). The notice must allow the tenant the usual amount of time in which to pay the balance, just as if the landlord had not accepted partial rent.

- A landlord who accepts partial rent after issuing a non-payment-of-rent notice does not waive the right to terminate if the parties agree in writing that accepting the rent money does not waive that right. The landlord would not have to issue a new nonpayment notice if the parties also agree in writing that the landlord can start a court eviction case without it after the remaining rent goes unpaid past a specified date.

- A landlord who accepts a federal rent subsidy as part payment of rent does not waive the right to evict a tenant who does not pay his or her share of the rent. This limitation also applies to any rental housing subsidy or fund administered by the Oregon Housing and Community Services Department.

- A last month's rent deposit collected at the beginning of the tenancy does not create a waiver of the right to terminate later, even if the deposit covers a period beyond the termination date in the notice.

- The disbursement to the landlord of rent money paid into court does not create a waiver of any right to terminate that the landlord might otherwise have.

- There is no waiver of the right to terminate if, within six days (seven days in a facility for a manufactured dwelling or floating home; see chapter 13) after the end of the correction period that applies to the for-cause notice given, the landlord refunds rent for the period beyond the termination date.

- A landlord does not waive by accepting rent prorated to the termination date in the notice.

- Once an eviction case on a for-cause notice has been started, the landlord does not lose the right to continue with the case by accepting rent from the tenant while the tenant remains at the rental after the notice expires so long as the landlord gives written notice that he or she is not waiving the right to terminate, and so long as the rent amount accepted does not cover a period later than the date the landlord gets it.

- When a landlord and a tenant have a written agreement that the periodic rent is to be paid not in a lump sum but in installments of a certain amount on certain dates, the landlord does not waive the right to terminate for non-payment by virtue of having accepted an earlier installment.

For space rentals in floating home or manufactured home facilities, there are two additional exceptions to the waiver rule. One involves a breach by the tenant in allowing his or her home to deteriorate or fall into disrepair or in failing to maintain the rental space. The other applies to terminations based on unacceptable tenant behavior. In those situations, the landlord must take some steps to avoid waiving his or her right to terminate. Before accepting the tenant's next rent payment, the landlord must give the tenant written notice about the problem behavior, describing the incident or course of conduct specifically, demanding that the tenant end the behavior, and stating that a reoccurrence of that conduct may result in termination of the tenancy. For an ongoing breach, the landlord's notice can be used in support of termination for up to one year.

Tenants need to be aware that a landlord's waiver of the right to terminate a tenancy for one cause does not necessarily keep the landlord from terminating for another cause or "no cause." For example, a landlord who has permitted loud parties may waive the right to terminate for similar disturbances but, by doing so, does not waive the right to evict for nonpayment of rent. There is generally no waiver defense against no-cause termination notices, although there may be other defenses.

11. New Tenancy Defense

Once in a while, a landlord will permit a tenant to remain in the rental even after a court judgment evicting the tenant. Or the landlord will present the tenant with a new and different rental agreement after giving the tenant a notice and after the termination date in the notice has gone by. If the parties agree that the tenant will stay for a while, the law will presume they have created a new tenancy, unless they agree otherwise. Having entered into a new agreement, the landlord can no longer rely on any notices from the earlier tenancy as the basis for an eviction.

12. Deterioration or Disrepair — Facility Space Rentals for Manufactured and Floating Homes Only

See ORS 90.632 and chapter 13 for a full discussion of the requirements for a termination based on this ground. Tenants may have several defenses specific to this kind of termination, such as —

- the dwelling is no more deteriorated than other units in the facility where tenancies are not being terminated;

- the corrections the landlord demands go beyond repair and maintenance;

- weather conditions make the kind of repair needed impossible to do within the time allotted and the landlord refuses to grant an extension;

- no qualified repair people are available within the time allotted;

- the landlord has known of the problem for more than a year, and so is obliged to give the tenant a longer time to correct the problem;

- the landlord's claim that the problem presents "imminent and serious risk" is exaggerated or unfounded;

- the landlord's claim is based only on the age, style, size, or construction of the manufactured home, not on its state of repair; and

- the tenant gave the landlord a notice of correction at least 14 days before the end of the correction period and the landlord did not respond in writing, so the landlord has waived the right to evict.

13. Repeated Late Payment — Facility Space Rentals for Manufactured and Floating Homes Only

Under certain circumstances, a facility landlord can terminate the tenancy of a home owner who rents space simply because the person has paid rent late. It is easy to imagine a situation in which a tenant might one time forget to pay until reminded, be hospitalized during the grace period in some other month, and away on vacation during the payment period later in the year. This very harsh rule has some limitations, fortunately, that tenants can use to defend against eviction for this reason. In order to terminate under this provision of the law, the facility landlord must first give the tenant at least three valid written nonpayment-of-rent notices in three of the preceding 12 months; and second, at least two of those notices (or a separate notice given with them or given shortly thereafter) in advance of the final notice must warn the tenant that a third such notice would result in the landlord's being able to terminate for cause and that the tenant would have no chance to correct the problem.

The landlord can issue the 30-day written notice based on the three post-notice payments either with or after the third nonpayment notice. The 30-day final notice must state the facts on which the landlord is relying to terminate the tenancy. In response, the tenant may be able to show one of more of these facts, any one of which would defeat an eviction:

- Rent that was overdue was paid before the landlord issued any nonpayment notice, or fewer than three such notices were issued.

- Because the landlord had violated the habitability or other provisions of ORLTA relating to facilities, no rent was due.

- The late payments of rent were not all within a 12-month period.

- The landlord did not include the necessary warnings on the first two nonpayment notices.

- One or more of the notices were given prematurely and so were not valid.

- The final notice does not state facts sufficient to notify the tenant of the reason for the termination.

- The landlord waived the right to use this kind of termination by accepting rent two or more times before issuing the final notice.

Landlords should be aware that tenants with cognitive impairments may be able to ask even at the eviction hearing for a reasonable accommodation for their disability if their disability kept them from being able to track their finances or dates. That accommodation could include the landlord's pre-notice verbal reminder to the tenant to pay the rent each month.

14. Crime Victim Defense

Landlords have the right (and even a duty to other tenants) to get rid of violent criminal tenants. In some cases, however, the victim of the violence is a member of the same household as the violent tenant. As a general matter of fairness, evicting someone for being a crime victim is problematic. In addition, the victims of certain kinds of crimes — domestic violence, stalking, and sexual assault — are overwhelmingly women. Thus, a landlord's practice or policy of terminating the tenancy of this kind of crime victim may be discriminatory because of the disparate impact the policy has. ORS 90.390 prohibits discrimination — deliberate or with an unequal impact — on the basis of sex.

Under ORLTA provisions enacted in 2003, a tenant who is the victim of this kind of crime should be able to defend against an eviction based on a for-cause notice alleging that the victim permitted the crime to occur in his or her rental. The use of a no-cause notice following an incident of violence against the tenant also will look suspicious in light of this change to the law.

However, the crime victim who takes no action to stop the occurrence of violence in the rental may lose the protection of the law. Therefore, the tenant who wants to use this defense should obtain an abuse protection order or a stalking order if possible, and arrange with the landlord to change door locks and oust the offender tenant. This tenant should get assistance from an attorney familiar with fair housing and domestic violence law.

15. Personal Injury, Property Damage, and Outrageous Conduct Defense

As discussed at the beginning of this chapter, a tenant can be evicted after a 24-hour notice without an opportunity to cure the problem if the tenant, the tenant's pet, or someone "under the tenant's control" causes or threatens injury to another person on the premises, acts with reckless disregard for the safety of others (such as throwing a refrigerator off a balcony), or behaves in an outrageous manner. ORLTA gives examples of outrageous behavior that include activities such as drug manufacturing, prostitution, and gambling rings. An act does not have to be criminal in order to constitute an "outrageous" act under the statute.

The tenant who receives this kind of notice may have one or more of these defenses:

- Tenant's "illegal" drugs are in fact legal medical marijuana.

- Tenant's illegal drugs are limited to less than one ounce of recreational marijuana.

- Tenant had no knowledge and no reason to know that a guest of the tenant would behave outrageously, and tenant has since told the guest never to return.

- Tenant's pet had never harmed anyone before, and tenant has removed the pet permanently since the incident that gave rise to the 24-hour notice.

- Tenant's behavior, although annoying, was not so serious as to warrant a 24-hour notice.

- The person who performed the outrageous act complained about was not the tenant and not a guest of the tenant.

- No outrageous act or violence or threat of violence or damage to property occurred. Landlord is mistaken or landlord is acting in bad faith.

Fortunately for landlords and for other tenants burdened by a tenant's illegal activities, proving a case for eviction based on a valid 24-hour notice is easier than proving that a crime was committed. In an eviction case, the judge or jury deciding the facts must believe only that it is more likely than not that the landlord's claims are true. A landlord acting in good faith to terminate a tenancy based on this kind of activity needn't worry about libel or slander so long as the accusations are made only in the notice and the legal papers the landlord files, and in the court proceeding itself.

16. Defenses to Drug-Free and Alcohol-Free Housing Evictions

The most obvious defense for a tenant who has violated one of the drug- and alcohol-free rules in this kind of housing is to stop the behavior immediately and show proof of the steps he or she took to address the problem.

For the tenant who has been erroneously accused of violating the drug- and alcohol-free rules, the most obvious defense is to provide proof to the court that the behavior complained of didn't happen. In many cases, a urinalysis or blood test conducted as soon as the tenant gets the notice can be helpful. So can the testimony of credible witnesses who can verify that the tenant has not been in violation.

Landlords of this special category of housing cannot use 48-hour notices to terminate tenancies for violations that are not drug and alcohol related. For all other kinds of causes for termination, these landlords must use the same kinds of notices that all other landlords use. A tenant who gets a 48-hour termination notice for some other kind of problem has a notice defense.

This kind of notice can be used only during the first two years of a tenancy. Whether a tenant in this type of housing wants to point out a longer residency may depend on the type of violation alleged — the rental agreement may still be terminable on 30 days' notice for a violation of an alcohol rule, with an opportunity to cure. A drug violation, on the other hand, may be of a type that would allow the landlord to evict on a 24-hour notice with no chance to correct the problem.

Only certain landlords are eligible to use this kind of notice: housing authorities and nonprofit agencies. A tenant has a notice defense against any other type of landlord that relies on this kind of notice.

Drug- and alcohol-free housing landlords may have given a 24-hour notice for a subsequent violation after the trial period allowing for it has ended, or they may have issued a 24-hour notice without first giving a 48-hour notice. These situations also give the tenant a procedural defense.

17. Illegal Subtenant Defense

The illegal subtenant may be able to say that the landlord knew of the person's presence at the rental and accepted rent from the real tenant or the subtenant without objecting to the person's occupancy at the time — a waiver defense.

In some cases, the subtenant is treated as "illegal" only after he or she asks for repairs. If the person is in fact a tenant, he or she can claim retaliation. This claim is stronger if the tenant can show that the landlord has a history of accepting new tenants so long as they don't ask for repairs.

It also is possible that the prior tenant did not have a written rental agreement, or had a rental agreement that did not prohibit subletting or assigning the tenancy. The subtenant may be able to get this information from the former tenant; if not, he or she will be forced to get the information from a landlord who may be unwilling to give it. In that case, the subtenant will need help from a lawyer in order to determine whether such a document exists, and, if so, obtain a copy of it from the landlord.

18. Evictions of Resident Managers

In some circumstances, a person who manages property for a landlord and receives reduced or free rent in return is not protected by ORLTA. The person is unprotected only if the person is an employee of the landlord and his or her right to occupancy is conditioned on employment in and around the rental property. A resident manager who answers an ad for such a job, signs an employment contract that says his or her right to occupy the premises is conditioned on employment and terminates when the employment ends, and moves into a unit specialized for a manager is excluded from ORLTA coverage. On the other hand, an existing tenant who accepts reduced rent in exchange for taking on some managerial duties without any express discussion of the impact of the work on his or her right to tenancy is clearly not excluded from ORLTA.

If a terminated resident manager is excluded from ORLTA and the landlord must evict him or her, the landlord must give at least 24 hours' written notice of termination of employment or the amount of time set forth in a written employment contract, whichever time is longer.

A manager who is not a protected tenant cannot use the retaliation defense that a tenant might use under appropriate circumstances. The manager may, however, have some recourse under the evolving law of wrongful discharge from employment. For example, the manager might have a public policy defense if he or she was dismissed for calling life-threatening fire hazards to the attention of the fire marshal after the landlord had made it clear nothing would be done otherwise. A manager who was fired for refusing to discriminate on the basis of race or ethnic origin is another example of a manager's public-policy defense.

Whether a manager-employee has notice defenses is likely to depend on the terms of any written contract and general employment law principles. Still, the notice must be consistent with this kind of eviction as well as with the contract itself.

A person who believes he or she is a tenant with managerial duties as opposed to a manager-employee excluded by ORLTA can claim tenancy as a defense to this kind of eviction. At trial the issue will be whether the parties understood when starting their work arrangement that the right to occupy was conditioned on employment or was merely payment for managerial work.

19. Farm Worker Employee Defense

Because of a long and ugly history of abuse of farm workers by their employers, Oregon employment law protects those workers who live on the employer's farmland (or nursery or dairy) from retaliation for exercising their rights to be paid for their work, for organizing a union, or getting legal advice, among other things. Tenant employees should get specific legal advice about any improper conduct by their landlord employer.

20. Military Service Defense

A member of the Oregon National Guard who is called into active service for at least 30 days may be able to get an eviction stayed for up to 90 days if the rent is no more than $1,200 per month and the unit is the home of the member's spouse, children, or other dependents. The tenant must be able to show that his or her ability to pay the rent is "materially affected" by his or her being called into active service.

Similar defenses are available to members of the national armed forces; members should get specific legal advice about their situations. Landlords who rent to members of the National Guard or the national armed forces should be aware of the limitations on eviction imposed by the federal Soldiers and Sailors' Civil Relief Act and a new section of ORLTA added in 2003. These provisions are designed to keep active-duty members from losing their homes, their jobs, and the right to appear in a court proceeding while they are on active duty. Landlords should get specific legal advice before proceeding with an eviction case against an active-duty military member.

21. Will Counterclaims Defeat Evictions?

In a counterclaim, a defendant asks the court for relief instead of or in addition to the relief the plaintiff wants. A landlord who is planning to evict should consider whether the tenant can and will counterclaim. A tenant facing eviction should decide whether a counterclaim is available and worth pursuing in the eviction case. In part, the answer will depend on whether the counterclaim can stop the eviction and how badly the tenant wants to stay in the rental. If the tenant is resigned to moving has counterclaims and believes the landlord will sue later for unpaid rent or damages, the tenant may want to wait until that case to raise counterclaims.

21.1 When can a tenant counterclaim?

Counterclaiming is difficult to do properly, and a tenant who tries to assert counterclaims without help from a lawyer is taking a significant risk. This situation is unfortunate because counterclaims are essential to the proper working of the law. It is through successful counterclaims that the tenant is able to force the landlord to make repairs to a dangerous or unhealthy home. (The alternative to counterclaims is a separate lawsuit, which is more costly, more complicated, and much slower.)

Counterclaims can result not only in a court order to a landlord to make repairs, stop harassment or retaliation, and follow the law, but also in an award for damages to the wronged tenant. Generally, damages are available to the tenant who has suffered harm as a result of a landlord's violations of the rental agreement or of ORLTA. In some instances, the tenant may lose the right to sue for damages later if the claims are not raised in response to the landlord's case. The law is unclear on this question; both tenants and landlords should get specific legal advice on this issue if at all possible.

Not all violations of the law provide for damages. An example is ORS 90.262, which makes improperly adopted rules unenforceable. This section simply keeps the landlord from using the rules against a tenant. But other provisions allow statutory damages — even if the tenant cannot prove any actual harm. The purpose of statutory damages is to deter future misconduct. In addition to violations of the rental agreement and ORLTA, violations of the Unlawful Trade Practices Act or Unlawful Debt Collection Practices Act can result in damage awards. Claims arising from the landlord-tenant relationship that are not based on a particular state statute, however, cannot be raised in an eviction case.

The list below includes most of the bases for counterclaims by a tenant in an eviction case. Statutory damage provisions are shown in parentheses.

(a) The landlord has been guilty of bad faith; ORS 90.130.

(b) The landlord has deliberately attempted to enforce a term in the rental agreement that he or she knows is prohibited by ORLTA; ORS 90.245. (The tenant is entitled to actual damages plus up to three months' rent.)

(c) The landlord has violated any provision of the rental agreement.

(d) The landlord has violated the habitability provisions or almost any of the other provisions of ORLTA.

(e) The landlord has knowingly failed to disclose in writing that the tenant is paying a utility for services that benefit another tenant or the landlord; ORS 90.315. (The tenant is entitled to the greater of twice the actual damages or one month's rent.)

(f) The landlord has deliberately or with gross negligence failed to provide an essential service; ORS 90.365. (Damages are limited to either reduction in rental value or cost of substitute housing; see chapter 6.)

(g) The landlord has locked the tenant out, shut off the utilities, or tried or threatened to do so, to force the tenant to leave; ORS 90.375. (The tenant is entitled to up to twice the actual damages or twice the monthly rent.)

(h) The landlord has abused the right of access; ORS 90.322. (The tenant is entitled to at least one month's rent.)

(i) The landlord has retaliated against the tenant by increasing rent, decreasing services, or threatening or attempting to evict; ORS 90.385, ORS 90.765. (The tenant is entitled to up to twice any actual damages or twice the monthly rent.)

(j) The landlord has wrongfully seized and retained the tenant's belongings; ORS 90.425, ORS 90.675. (The tenant is relieved of any obligations for unpaid rent and is entitled to recover up to twice any actual damages.)

(k) The landlord has violated the Unlawful Trade Practices Act with conduct that is not covered by ORLTA. (The tenant is entitled to at least $200 for damages.)

(l) The landlord has violated the Unlawful Debt Collection Practices Act. (The tenant is entitled to at least $200 for damages.)

(m) The landlord has engaged in unlawful discrimination; ORS 90.390.

Note: Space-renting home owners in manufactured and floating home facilities have slightly different claims and remedies in some cases.

Not every violation gives rise to a counterclaim. The tenant must be able to show that the violation caused some kind of harm, unless the provision violated allows statutory damages without proof of harm. Most violations of ORLTA involve a loss in the rental value of the premises, and this kind of harm is enough to support a counterclaim.

Tenants (and their guests) can recover damages through a counterclaim for personal injuries, lost or damaged personal belongings, and any financial loss or expense caused by any of the violations. However, under ORLTA, tenants have a duty to cut their losses, or "mitigate the damages." For example, a leak in the ceiling gets the tenant's sofa wet. If the tenant leaves the sofa under the leak, and sofa is eventually ruined, the tenant cannot ascribe all of the blame to the landlord for the ruined sofa.

Although damages are not available for emotional distress resulting from merely negligent habitability violations, a tenant may recover emotional distress damages in appropriate cases resulting from deliberate violations of the lockout, shutoff, and retaliation provisions. The courts have not yet ruled whether this kind of damages is available for deliberate habitability violations.

If the tenant wins the eviction case based on a counterclaim, the court can make the landlord pay for the tenant's attorney fees in an amount set by the court. The court can award attorney fees against the tenant if the landlord wins.

21.2 When can a counterclaim allow a tenant to stay?

Whether or not a counterclaim can defeat a landlord's attempt to evict depends on the nature of both the eviction case and the counterclaim.

Counterclaims are most useful in nonpayment-of-rent eviction cases. If the counterclaim "offsets" (is as much as or is greater than) all rent claimed, the tenant should win. Just as important, a tenant who pays rent into court to support a counterclaim in this kind of case will have the benefit of the "second chance" provisions described in chapter 6. Thus, the tenant can win the eviction case even if the court finds the counterclaim damages are too small to offset all of the rent claimed. If the rent paid into court covers the balance owing, or if the tenant adds enough to the money paid into court to pay all rent the court decides is due, the tenant will get to stay in the rental. Unless the landlord can prove the tenant has acted in bad faith, a tenant who pays rent into court to support a counterclaim cannot be evicted if the rent paid into court covers any balance found to be due. However, if at the end of trial, the tenant has to add to the money originally paid into court, the landlord is not responsible for the tenant's attorney fees.

A judge cannot decide independently to require the tenant to pay rent into court solely to support a counterclaim. The judge can do so only if asked by the landlord or the tenant. Whether or not to ask for the court's permission is a strategy decision, best made after consulting an attorney.

Paying rent into court means that the tenant will have no access to that money unless and until the court orders the release of the money. The court may decide to release the money to the landlord, or a portion to each party. Even then, the county's finance department may take two to three weeks to process any refund the court awarded to the tenant. Not every tenant can afford to risk being without cash for that period of time. Still, if the tenant has to pay current rent into court anyway so as to get a delay in the trial date, the extra burden of paying back rent into court may not present much more of a problem.

21.3 How to decide whether or not to counterclaim

A tenant may want to file a counterclaim even if it is not based on facts that amount to a defense to eviction. The counterclaim may be the fastest way to collect damages from the landlord even if the tenant loses the right to the rental, and it can be very useful in settlement negotiations. Furthermore, the court of appeals has held that if a tenant wins money on a counterclaim, the landlord cannot recover attorney fees from the tenant even if the landlord is successful in having the court evict the tenant.

Every tenant considering counterclaiming must weigh these considerations in light of his or her own situation. Still, as a general rule, it is possible to conclude that —

- the tenant whose top priority is to stay in the rental usually is in a better position if she or he counterclaims; and

- if the tenant's defenses to eviction are weak, or if the tenant's top priority is to get damages on facts that are not closely related to the landlord's right to terminate the tenancy, it is usually better to file a damage claim separately.

If a landlord files a lawsuit for back rent later, the former tenant can raise counterclaims and recoupments then, and, after moving out, cannot be ordered to pay rent into court in such a case.

22. Whether and How to Defend Against Eviction

Should a tenant faced with eviction try to fight it? The tenant who wants to remain in the unit and who has legitimate defenses to eviction will probably say yes. Can that tenant handle the case without help from a lawyer if necessary? That's a much harder question. There are other considerations to weigh, too.

The tenant who does not contest the case — by filing a legal answer — will be evicted by default: the landlord will get the rental home back, the costs of filing and serving the court papers, and a "prevailing party fee" of more than $200. Altogether, the money the landlord is awarded will be around $500. However, when the tenant does not go to court, the landlord is not entitled to attorney fees. The tenant with a record of eviction may have more difficulty renting from another landlord.

In the rare case where a landlord combines a complaint for eviction with other claims for damage or back rent (in which case the tenant has up to 30 days to respond in regular court, or 7 days in justice court), the tenant who does not contest will face a judgment for the full amount of the money claimed as well as an eviction. In that kind of case, the landlord can be awarded attorney fees even if the tenant does not file an answer.

A tenant who has resources should know that a landlord, like any other creditor, may be able to take some of the resources after getting a judgment for money; for example, by garnishing money in a bank account. The tenant who has very little income and assets usually is protected from having to turn over resources to creditors. Oregon's "exemption" statutes list certain basic property that creditors with judgments cannot take — such as government benefits including Social Security and unemployment payments, a certain amount of cash, a vehicle, work tools (up to a certain value), clothing, some jewelry and heirlooms, and other things.

While the exemption statutes protect low-income tenants from money judgments, nothing protects them from a lawful judgment of eviction. A tenant who lets the case be decided by default will likely have only four to six days in which to move out afterward. Thus, the tenant who has no legitimate defense to the eviction may want to show up at the first-appearance time solely to ask the judge for some extra time to move. If the tenant does not file an answer, the judge should not award the landlord any attorney fees (ORS 105.137). Courts that use mediation in conjunction with their eviction cases may charge the tenant a filing fee if the two sides come to an agreement that they want the court to honor or enforce. A tenant who is concerned about when and how a fee is charged in this situation should get information from the local court clerk or eviction-mediation program.

The tenant who wants to fight an eviction must not ignore any court papers that he or she receives. It is not necessary for the papers to come personally to the tenant — they can be mailed and posted on the rental entrance and still be effective. And it is foolish to decide the papers don't "count" because they have been filled out improperly — having a lawyer argue the technicalities is much more likely to be successful at the beginning of the case than it would be later, when the court has already signed a judgment of eviction.

It is essential for the tenant or the tenant's lawyer to show up promptly in court at the first-appearance time. Many tenants have arrived at the courthouse 15 minutes past the time to appear, only to discover that they have already been evicted by default. Only in rare instances — such as when the tenant is in a hospital emergency room — have judges been willing to extend the time for an appearance by a few hours, or agreed to a telephone appearance so long as the tenant's court papers were filed by the end of the same day. Tenants with unreliable transportation — or unreliable friends who have offered to transport them — should give themselves lots of time to arrive at the courthouse early. Courthouses are busy places. There is almost never a place to park nearby, and there is almost always a line of people standing at the information window (if there even is an information window!) trying to find out where they are supposed to go for their court appearances.

The tenant that has an attorney should get the court papers to the lawyer as soon as possible. Some judges may give a tenant an extra day or two in which to obtain a lawyer before filing an answer, but they are not obliged to do so (ORS 105.140). In any event, a tenant can file a very simple answer at the first appearance, then amend it before the trial. A tenant that does not have a lawyer can even bring up other defenses for the first time at trial (ORS 105.137). The landlord has the right to ask for a postponement to prepare further if that happens.

22.1 Is a lawyer necessary?

Is a lawyer necessary for the defense against an eviction? The case can become fairly complicated and technical, and attorney assistance can become very expensive — upwards of $1,000. Even the winner of the case who gets awarded attorney fees from the loser may have trouble collecting the money. Still, the odds of winning go up dramatically for those who are represented. (Chapter 15 lists a number of ways for tenants to find lawyers who can help them.)

Inevitably, there will be tenants who have legitimate defenses to eviction but who cannot get representation. If you are one of these tenants, and you decided to go forward on your own, the information in this book should be valuable to you. It is important to note that the law may have changed by the time you go to court, and that what may seem like small differences in facts can make big differences in outcomes.

22.2 Going to court without legal representation

As described earlier in this chapter, the case officially begins when the landlord files a complaint in court. Someone then mails and delivers or posts a copy of the complaint to the tenant, who must show up at the first-appearance time if he or she wants to contest the case. It is crucial to read the court papers carefully, not only to find out when to be in court but also to find out the court's policy on recording trials. In some counties, courts record certain kinds of trials only if one of the parties asks for the recording. If no one does, and the judge makes a wrong decision at the end of the case, the losing party will be unable to appeal anything decided in the trial.

It is a good idea for the tenant to get an answer form from the court clerk's office as soon as possible, and to have it (and a request for a filing-fee deferral if needed) ready at the first appearance. At the first appearance, the tenant asks for a trial and gives the court the fee deferral request and the answer form. The tenant must give the landlord a copy of the answer form at the same time, marked "True copy" and signed by the tenant. The landlord does not get a copy of the fee deferral request. Sometimes the judge will look at the fee deferral form or the answer form right away; sometimes the judge will tell the tenant to take the forms to the court clerk.

The judge may try to get the parties to come to an agreement, or may send the parties to a mediator to try to come to an agreement. If there is no agreement, the parties must go to the court clerk's office to set up their trial date. The landlord must pay additional filing fees and the tenant will have to pay fees as well — unless the court defers or waives the filing fee. The tenant has until the end of the clerk's workday to pay any money the court requires. Do not assume that the clerk's office stays open until 5 p.m. In many counties, it doesn't. The tenant must fill out another court form called a "proof of service" telling when, where, and how the tenant gave a copy of the answer to the landlord. That form is left in the court file (see Sample 20).

Sample 21 shows a version of an answer in a nonpayment-of-rent eviction case in which a tenant says the landlord is not entitled to the rent because the rental needed many repairs. (**Note:** The actual court forms will look different, but the language will be similar.) Tenants with different or additional defenses would complete other sections of the answer form.

To counterclaim, the tenant must change the form answer, clearly designating a section for counterclaims. If there are additional counterclaims that do not fit on the form, another page can be added. The first page should say the counterclaims are continued on the next page, and the next page should say the counterclaims are continued from the first page and should have the case number on it. (Sample 22 shows a form answer with a counterclaim, in a case for nonpayment of rent.) The tenant should use the same facts that were used for counterclaims as defenses as well. In the nonpayment-of-rent context, any counterclaim the tenant has for damages arising under the rental agreement or ORLTA can be used to offset any rent claimed by the landlord in the nonpayment case.

When writing counterclaims or explaining portions of the form answer, the tenant must be aware that some words have special meanings when used in court papers. For example, the word "answer" has a very different meaning in court than it does in real life. In another example, a tenant who wants to challenge the way a notice was "served" should know that saying the notice was served can mean that it was delivered personally to the tenant. If a notice was mailed but not posted to the entrance of the rental as required in some situations, the tenant is safer to describe the

SAMPLE 20
PROOF OF SERVICE

I, Leonard Tenant, hereby say that on July 18, 20--, I handed a true, correct copy of the within Answer to the plaintiff in the clerk's office of this court.

Leonard Tenant

Subscribed and sworn to this 18th day of July 20--, at Eugene, Oregon.

J. M. Notary
Notary Public
My commission expires 7/21/-

process just that way; for example, "the landlord mailed the termination notice of December 1, 20--, but did not attach a copy to the entrance of my apartment as required by law." A wise tenant who can afford to do so will at the very least have a lawyer look over the tenant's proposed language before the tenant finalizes the answer and counterclaims. Having a lawyer read it may help the tenant from being trapped by legalese.

Some additional "dos and don'ts" when answering or counterclaiming:

(a) Just state the facts, not your reaction to them.

(b) Make sure that all statements are truthful, and not exaggerated to impress the court — the time to try to win sympathy for your side of the case is in the courtroom when summing up your case.

(c) Date and sign the answer, file the original, and, unless you hand a copy of the answer to the landlord in the courtroom in front of the judge, stating that you are doing that, attach a "proof of service" to the original describing how and when you sent a true copy to the landlord.

SAMPLE 21
FORM ANSWER TO EVICTION CASE

I deny that the plaintiff is entitled to possession because:

 X The landlord did not make the repairs.

List any repair problems: Toilet fills so slowly it can be used only once a day; no heat; no working lock and resulting loss of $400 property due to theft.

 X The landlord is attempting to evict me because of my complaints (or the eviction is otherwise retaliatory).

___ The eviction notice is wrong.

List any other defenses: _____

_____

_____

I may be entitled as the prevailing party to recover attorney fees from plaintiff if I obtain legal services to defend this action pursuant to ORS 90.255.

I ask that the plaintiff take nothing by the complaint and that I be awarded my costs and disbursements and lawyer fees, if applicable, or a prevailing party fee.

July 18, 20--
Date

Leonard Tenant
Signature of defendant

SAMPLE 22
COUNTERCLAIMS

List any other defenses: I COUNTERCLAIM for $400 because of the bad lock, $300 because of the defective toilet *(lost rental value)*, and $800 because of no heat *(lost rental value, discomfort)*. I ask that the court award me judgment against the plaintiff for $1,500.

(d) If you want a jury trial (inadvisable for either party without a lawyer to handle the case), you must write "jury trial requested" on the answer form. A jury trial involves additional costs. Local court rules (called supplemental local rules or SLRs) may require you to take additional steps to assure that you get a jury. You can read the rules at the law library or online.

22.3 Judges

It is a fact of life that judges, like everyone else, have preconceived notions about fairness. In a few instances, that will mean the judge is hostile to a tenant's rights, to the point where the tenant will almost certainly lose an eviction case in that particular judge's courtroom. (One such judge has been nicknamed by lawyers "the landlord's best friend.") Fortunately, there is usually a way to avoid a very prejudiced judge.

Neither side gets to "pick" the judge who will hear the case. But both sides have the right to ask — by filing a motion — that a certain judge (up to two judges) not decide the case if they believe that the judge scheduled to hear the case cannot be impartial by reason of prejudice. A concerned party does not have to prove prejudice, but must have reasonable grounds to believe the judge will not be fair. The party who files the motion must do so before the assigned judge has made any ruling in the case beyond whether to grant a filing fee waiver or deferral. It may be best to make a motion for a change of judge before the first appearance; to be sure, ask the court clerk how and when cases get assigned. The tenant who is uncertain about when in the process to ask for a different judge can ask for a change of judge at the first appearance by saying, "Your honor, I would like to file an affidavit to disqualify a judge." The tenant must then file the formal motion and affidavit with the clerk, giving the landlord a copy of the papers. (**Note:** The landlord's copy must say "True Copy" and be signed by the tenant, and the tenant must file a "proof of service" with the court clerk.)

How can someone know in advance if there is a judge that should be avoided? Once in a while a court clerk may say whether some judges get "affidavited" or "recused" often, and by which side in the case. Sometimes a look at a handful of past court case files (at least in counties with only a few judges) will turn up a name or names. Or a party can ask a lawyer familiar with land-lord-tenant practice. See Sample 23 for a general idea of what such a motion would look like, but know that the uniform trial court rules and some local rules require the use of a specific format.

On a rare occasion, the judge at the first appearance may suggest that the parties "just have the trial right now." Neither side is likely to have all of its evidence or witnesses — or perhaps even the party's lawyer — at the first appearance. It is especially important for the tenant to point out that he or she needs to notify witnesses when to appear, and to decline to have an immediate hearing. Nonetheless, it is evidently not unlawful for court clerks to set the trial for the following day; a 15-day delay is the maximum amount of time permitted between the first appearance and trial.

22.4 Pretrial settlement and trial

At the first appearance or very soon afterward, the parties will find out when their trial is scheduled. In some counties, the parties are sent to a mediator to help them resolve their dispute. If a mediator is involved, the parties frequently come to an agreement. They do not have to agree, but if they do, they must notify the court about their agreement. The agreement may be to dismiss the case; dismiss the case so long as one or both of the parties do certain things they have promised, usually by a certain date; or enter a judgment of restitution, or restitution conditioned on the failure of the tenant to do what he or she has agreed to do by a certain date. All of these outcomes are different kinds of "stipulated orders" (temporary, while the case formally remains open) or "stipulated judgments" (the final, permanent decision). Sample 24 shows an example of a stipulation for a judgment; this example becomes a judgment as soon as the judge signs it. A dismissal means that the tenant is not evicted. Sample 25 shows a generalized example of the dismissal form, which the landlord files with the court to obtain the dismissal. A judgment of restitution means that the landlord gets the property back and the tenant is evicted.

Oregon's eviction statutes have special procedures for landlords and tenants who work out an agreement pretrial, with or without the help of a mediator. If the parties have stipulated to an order requiring either side to do anything, the judge has no discretion to change the agreement or refuse to accept the agreement (ORS 105.145). A landlord who gets a tenant to agree to something that would be unconscionable if it were in a rental agreement, though, will not be able to enforce that part of the agreement. The

SAMPLE 23
MOTION AND AFFIDAVIT FOR CHANGE OF JUDGE

IN THE CIRCUIT COURT OF THE STATE OF OREGON
FOR THE COUNTY OF MULTNOMAH

J. Landlord,	)	Case No. <u>1234565</u>
Plaintiff,	)	MOTION AND
vs.	)	AFFIDAVIT FOR
L. Tenant,	)	CHANGE OF JUDGE
Defendant.	)	

STATE OF OREGON   )
ss.
COUNTY OF MULTNOMAH)

I, Leonard Tenant, hereby say that I am the defendant in the above-entitled matter, and that I believe that I cannot have a fair and impartial trial before the Honorable*[name of judge]*, who is assigned to hear this case. I request that another judge be assigned to hear this case.

This motion and affidavit are filed in good faith and not for the purpose of delay.

L. Tenant

Defendant

SUBSCRIBED AND SWORN TO before me this 14th of May, 20--, at Portland, Oregon.

I. M. Public

Notary Public
My commission
expires 7/21/--

Note: This sample does not reflect the style requirements of state or local court rules.

JUDGMENT BY STIPULATION

IN THE CIRCUIT COURT OF THE STATE OF OREGON
FOR THE COUNTY OF MULTNOMAH

J. Landlord,	)	Case No. <u>1234565</u>
Plaintiff,	)	JUDGMENT BY
vs.	)	STIPULATION
L. Tenant,	)	
Defendant.	)	

Plaintiff and defendant hereby agree that judgment may be entered in this action as follows:

1. Plaintiff shall have restitution of the subject premises, with execution stayed through July 15, 20--;

2. Each party releases the other from any and all liability arising with respect to the subject tenancy;

3. Each party will bear its own costs.

J. Landlord
Plaintiff
June 10, 20--

L. Tenant
Defendant
June 10, 20--

IT IS SO ORDERED AND ADJUDGED

I. M. Judge
Judge

Note: This sample does not reflect the style requirements of state or local court rules.

court of appeals has determined that this kind of agreement in effect creates a new rental agreement, subject to all of the requirements and limitations of ORLTA.

What kinds of things are appropriate for settlement? Generally, it is advantageous for tenants to push for a court order of dismissal in lieu of a judgment of eviction. That is true even if the

SAMPLE 25
DISMISSAL FORM

IN THE CIRCUIT COURT OF THE STATE OF OREGON
FOR THE COUNTY OF MULTNOMAH

J. Landlord,	)	Case No. <u>1234565</u>
Plaintiff,	)	MOTION FOR
vs.	)	DISMISSAL
L. Tenant,	)	
Defendant.	)	

J. Landlord, plaintiff in the above-entitled action,
hereby requests an order of dismissal and a judgment
of nonsuit.

Dated: July 24, 20--

J. Landlord

Plaintiff

Note: This sample does not take into account the style requirements of various
state and local court rules.

tenant agrees to move out right away, because later landlords will
be more willing to rent to them. Tenants can also benefit if landlords are willing not to ask for judgments for filing fees and costs.
Sometimes landlords are willing to make agreements like this if
they fear they may be found liable for damages to the tenant. So
tenants can agree not to pursue the landlord later for damages in
order to avoid a judgment. There are many other ways the parties
can work together for their mutual advantage.

The following example shows how the pretrial settlement
procedure works:

> **Example:** A landlord starts to evict a tenant for non-
> payment of rent after the tenant has lost her job. With
> no income, the tenant is unable to pay her rent. At the
> time of the first appearance, the tenant has a new job
> that should make it possible for her to pay rent in the
> future and to make up the back rent. The landlord

agrees to stop the eviction, provided that the tenant pays a certain amount at designated times to catch up on the rent. The parties take their agreement to the judge, who signs the stipulated order. If the tenant does not abide by the agreement, the landlord can quickly return to court without paying any new filing fees to ask for a judgment of restitution that will evict the tenant. The tenant is entitled to notice of the landlord's return to court and an opportunity to challenge the landlord's position.

There are limits to what the landlord and tenant can agree to, if the landlord wants to convert the stipulated order into a judgment of restitution (in addition to the unenforceable-rule issue mentioned above). They can agree to —

- the tenant's conduct or performance of certain actions for no more than six months from the date of the order;

- payment of past due rent and other past due money on a schedule listed in the order for no more than six months;

- payment of future rent on a schedule set out in the order for three months from the date of the order; and

- payment of court costs and attorney fees according to a schedule in the order.

The landlord cannot use a post-settlement judgment of restitution to force out the tenant for reasons other than violations of these provisions within the time stated. After the time limits set out above, a violation of the agreement by the tenant will mean that the landlord must use the usual methods to start the eviction process again (e.g., nonpayment-of-rent, other for-cause notices).

When the parties have entered into a settlement, the order signed by the court must say that the case will be dismissed automatically after 12 months without notice to either side.

If the tenant does not abide by the settlement agreement, the landlord files with the court clerk a statutory form called an affidavit of noncompliance, along with a copy of the stipulated order and any documentation of the actual terms of the settlement agreement. The affidavit of noncompliance must describe how the tenant did not comply with the terms of that agreement. The court will then sign a judgment of restitution; the court clerk will send a notice of restitution to the tenant, along with copies of the underlying documents. Because some landlords have submitted affidavits falsely charging noncompliance by the tenant, 2003 legislation requires that the tenant have an opportunity to delay restitution long enough to get a hearing on the landlord's claim of noncompliance. How the courts handle this will be laid out in the uniform trial court rules, or local court rules, or both.

The court clerk's office provides a form for the tenant, called "defendant's request for hearing to contest an affidavit of noncompliance" (ORS 105.148). The tenant must explain on the form how the tenant complied with the order or explain why the tenant should not be required to comply. This kind of reason would include the landlord's failure to do what the landlord had agreed in the stipulated judgment. The form must be filed before the clerk issues a writ of execution for the sheriff to enforce the judgment of eviction. The clerk must set a hearing "as soon as practicable," notifying the parties by mail or even by facsimile (ORS 105.149). Whatever else the court rules may say about how the tenant can get a hearing, it is clear that the hearing must occur very quickly.

The noncompliance hearing can cover whether or not the parties did what they were supposed to under the stipulation only. ORS 105.149 lays out the scope of the hearing. The following questions may be answered at a noncompliance hearing:

- Did the landlord comply with the requirements of the order that was a precondition to what the tenant was required to do?

- Did the tenant comply with the order?

- Did the parties modify the court order and then comply with the modified order?

- Did one side unfairly prevent the other side from complying with the order?

- Was the agreement entered into in good faith?

- Is the agreement unconscionable against the tenant?

- Does the conduct or performance by a tenant — when noncompliance is based on conduct or performance — constitute a "material breach" of the stipulation or ORLTA that requires the landlord to have good cause to terminate the tenancy?

- Does the tenant who entered into a stipulation to pay future rent have a claim for money that arose after the entry of the stipulation that would provide a defense to nonpayment?

If the tenant does not appear at the hearing, the court clerk will issue the writ of execution to the sheriff immediately. If the judge at the hearing rules in favor of the tenant, the court will set aside the judgment. The case will then be treated like other cases that have not yet had trials. If the judge rules in favor of the landlord, the clerk will issue a writ of execution no sooner than 24 hours after the judgment.

22.4a Gathering evidence

As soon as a tenant decides that he or she is going to fight an eviction, there are several things the tenant must do. One of those things is to gather evidence. Evidence is sometimes the testimony of witnesses. Some witnesses may come to court voluntarily, but some cannot or will not. Those witnesses will need to be subpoenaed. Subpoena forms are available from the court clerk; those who are subpoenaed must be offered a fee and their mileage at the time they get the subpoena (the court clerk can confirm the current rates). The court cannot defer or waive these fees. Building inspectors and other agency officials almost always require subpoenas before they will appear in court.

22.4b Witnesses

Witnesses need to have knowledge of the things that need to be proved. Sometimes the parties themselves will be the only witnesses needed because they have personal knowledge of all of the relevant facts. Normally, only a person with personal knowledge of things being testified about can testify about those things. However, either side can testify about what the other party has said. For example, if a neighbor heard a landlord say he started the eviction case because the tenant who complained about the leaky roof was a troublemaker, the neighbor can talk about what she heard if the landlord claims he was not retaliating for lawful tenant conduct.

Witnesses to the reduction in rental value of a rental brought about by habitability problems should read the description of how to describe the reduction in the habitability defense section (see section 9). A tenant must provide evidence of how much the rental value diminished in order for a court to calculate how much of the rent was due. Simply showing the problems is not enough. The tenant must show how and to what extent the problem interfered with a safe, normal life.

Some courts allow people who are not lawyers a little freedom from the rules of evidence, but tenants should not be surprised to find out they are not allowed to ask leading questions of their own witnesses. It is entirely proper — and a good idea — to review the questions with the witnesses in advance of the trial.

22.4c Courtroom etiquette

Another important thing to do is to watch other people's trials before going to one's own trial. Every trial follows certain procedures, such as where the parties sit, who goes first, how witnesses are called, when the parties can ask questions and when they can make arguments, and how they get documents and photographs into the court record (so that the judge must take them into account when making a ruling).

One thing that can be observed in any kind of court proceeding (and real life, for that matter) is the importance of good manners. People who go into the courtroom with the attitude that the judge is the enemy forget that it makes no sense to be nasty to someone who has the discretion to help them. It is important to know that when appearing in court one should make an effort to dress simply and conservatively; men who refuse to remove hats do not earn the judge's respect.

The procedure generally is that everyone in the courtroom stands when the judge enters. Parties stand up to object to questions from the other party that they believe violate rules of evidence. They ask the judge for permission to approach a witness on the stand in order to show the witness a document that they want to use as evidence in their case. They give the other side a copy of the same document. When the witness has finished with the document, the party who wants the document in evidence must say, "I offer exhibit number ___ into evidence," and wait to hear any objection from the other side and a ruling from the judge before giving the document to the court's clerk. Before the trial gets underway, the parties are supposed to label and number any documents they intend to use as evidence. The judge's assistant generally has the necessary labels.

When an eviction trial starts, the landlord goes first. The tenant can cross-examine the landlord's witnesses, but is generally better off just offering testimony when it is the tenant's turn to put on his or her side of the case. When the tenant and tenant's witnesses testify, the landlord's side can cross-examine what they say. When the testimony is done, each side has a brief opportunity to explain to the judge how the facts point to its position in the case, and to point out provisions of the law that support that position. Few judges have much experience dealing with ORLTA, so showing them the sections of the law that support a position can be very helpful to them.

23. After a Judgment of Eviction (Restitution)

An eviction judgment does not give the landlord or any other private individual the right to lock out a tenant, seize the tenant's belongings, or turn off the utilities. Although the abandoned property law applies when a tenant is gone continuously from the rental for at least seven days after the eviction judgment (see chapter 11), in all other cases the landlord must use the sheriff's department to remove the tenant permanently.

To get help from the sheriff, the landlord must ask the court clerk for an "execution of judgment" after the court judgment is final. The sheriff's department or a process server then gives the tenant a notice, or, in the tenant's absence, posts a notice on the rental that the landlord is entitled to have the property back and that, unless the tenant gets out and takes his or her belongings within four days, the sheriff will return to remove the tenant forcibly if necessary. There is a fee for the service of the notice.

There is an additional fee for the sheriff to return to remove the tenant. The sheriff gives a final trespass-eviction notice to the tenant or posts the rental with the notice. If the tenant attempts to come back to the rental after the final removal, the tenant can be arrested for trespassing. The landlord assumes responsibility for the tenant's belongings, as described in chapter 11.

24. Can the Tenant Appeal?

A tenant who believes that a trial court was wrong not to allow the tenant to remain in the rental or not to award the tenant damages may be able to appeal. An appeal can change the result of the case or simply give the tenant a chance for a new trial. An appeal almost always requires a lawyer's help. The steps involved depend on whether the trial was in justice court or regular court, and on what the tenant wants.

The tenant must in any case file an "undertaking" or deposit a certain amount of money into court. An undertaking is the promise by some third person to pay whatever amounts the undertaking covers if the appeal is unsuccessful. The minimum amount of an undertaking is $500. The person who signs the undertaking can be an agent for a bonding company or a private individual with enough assets to cover the amounts estimated. The court can authorize a tenant to pay cash into court instead of an undertaking. The court can waive or reduce the undertaking on the ground of the tenant's indigency.

The tenant who wants to stay in the rental while appealing a regular court eviction must act very quickly to "stay" (stop) the court's decision to evict. In this situation, the tenant is looking at an additional undertaking, one large enough to cover damages, costs, and disbursements that may be awarded on appeal, as above, as well as any damages arising from destruction of or harm to the property during the appeal and the value of the use and occupancy of the rental during the appeal. The court usually will consider that the amount of damage to the property will be minimal given that the tenant would have to live in any damage he or she were to cause, and generally will permit the tenant simply to pay rent into court as the rent becomes due during the pendency of the appeal. The tenant who does not want to stay in the rental and wants only damages will not need a stay, and so will not need to pay this additional amount.

Like trial courts, the court of appeals charges filing fees. The fee in 2004 was $150. The appellate courts defer or waive the fee for very low-income appellants. The winner of an appeal is generally awarded these costs, along with attorney fees and prevailing party fees. Tenant money paid for an undertaking comes back to the tenant if the tenant wins. The landlord gets the undertaking funds if the landlord wins. Any rent paid into court is released according to the court's decision — to one party or the other, or part to each.

For the tenant who wants to stay, it is essential to get a copy of the tape recording of the trial immediately. The tenant who wants legal advice about the chances of winning an appeal will have to give the tape to an attorney to review. The "stay" must go into effect before the sheriff's department executes on the judgment, so listening to the tapes and submitting the notice of appeal and the motion for stay usually must be accomplished within four days.

The tenant who appeals a justice court eviction judgment has a slightly different task: the appeal is for a new trial in regular court. To get a stay, the tenant must file an undertaking or deposit cash to cover costs, disbursements, and any judgment that might be warded the landlord on appeals. This amount includes a judgment for attorney fees. For the tenant who is not seeking a stay of the eviction but wants only damages, the undertaking is smaller because it needs to cover only costs and disbursements, not attorney fees. The trial court has the power to waive or reduce the undertaking for good cause, including the tenant's indigency.

There are some typical errors that trial courts make and that tenants should be able to appeal successfully. Tenants should be able to appeal the —

- court's insistence that tenants make habitability complaints in writing,

- ruling that tenants show evidence of actual damages before awarding statutory damages of one month's rent after an unlawful landlord entry,

- refusal to listen to the tenant's evidence or claims,

- demand that tenants pay rent into court when there is no statutory basis to do so, and

- refusal to award attorney fees to tenants' lawyers when fees should be awarded.

CHAPTER NINE

EMERGENCIES, THE POLICE, AND TEMPORARY RESTRAINING ORDERS

Landlords and tenants both have access to emergency remedies in extreme circumstances. Although this process is much faster than most judicial proceedings, it can seem excruciatingly slow to those affected by emergency situations.

Landlords have recourse to 24-hour notices of eviction in extreme cases (see chapter 8). There are at least two other steps a landlord can take in serious situations. A landlord who reasonably believes the tenant has committed a crime or is committing a crime (e.g., drug activity, prostitution, domestic violence, or serious property damage) at the rental should consider calling the police. Calling the police is not a shortcut around the need to evict a dangerous tenant; however, it may be a faster way to prevent further harm while the eviction is pending.

The police are trained to intervene in volatile situations. Whether they will make an arrest will vary with the jurisdiction, the available jail space, and individual officers' discretion. A warning can sometimes be effective. In any event, an arrested tenant is usually soon released and has every right to return "home" until the tenancy is officially terminated by the court or by the tenant's intentional abandonment or relinquishment of the rental. (A tenant who is in jail is rarely in a position to "abandon" merely by not returning to the premises, but there is no reason a summons and complaint for eviction cannot be served in jail in addition to the regular method.)

If the police won't help, contact a mental health employee or social worker, a domestic violence victims' assistance program, or a probation officer if the problem tenant has one. In short, contact any professional who might be able to intervene.

There is still one other recourse — the same one that is available to a tenant who has been locked out by the landlord or whose utility services have been unlawfully shut off: the temporary restraining order (TRO). The TRO is available only for extreme circumstances: the threatened loss or injury must be "irreparable" without the order, and legal remedies must be "inadequate" to compensate after the fact for the threatened harm or loss. The primary objective of a TRO is to invoke the court's power to forbid specific conduct. For example, if a landlord obtains a TRO ordering a violent tenant to refrain from threatening behavior before trial, the landlord can be fairly sure of a police response if the order is violated. A TRO is not appropriate just because the tenant has stopped paying the rent or has no money to pay a judgment. The landlord could have avoided this problem by obtaining sufficient security deposits at the beginning of the tenancy.

Getting a TRO can be complicated and expensive, because it is not the kind of remedy someone is likely to be able to get without the help of a lawyer. In fact, in Oregon, it is not even possible to get injunctive relief (an order to force a party to stop its wrongful behavior from now into the future) in small claims court.

Gathering the evidence the lawyer will need for the case can minimize your costs: interview the people who have first-hand knowledge of the problem and how serious it is. Get their names, addresses, and phone numbers, as some of them may be needed as witnesses in court. At the hearing, the landlord and witnesses must show why waiting for a judgment of eviction is not an adequate remedy.

Think of as many ways as possible to notify the tenant about the hearing date, as it will likely occur within a day or two, sometimes before the person would normally be able to find out about the case. The tenant has the right to come to the hearing and argue that a TRO is not appropriate in the case.

Although a bond or undertaking (the payment or assurance of payment) is normally required to make a temporary restraining order enforceable, it is not needed if the petitioner merely wants to protect a person from violent or threatening behavior or to prevent unlawful conduct. This question shouldn't come up if a judge decides to enjoin a tenant from threatening to beat up his or her landlord or other tenants. However, if the landlord wants more, such as an order that the violent member of the tenant's household stay away from the premises until trial, there is at least an argument that the normal undertaking is required. (In the case of a tenant who is violent against an adult in the tenant's own household, the landlord may be able to get the offender out more quickly — see chapter 8 for removal of domestic-violence perpetrators.)

For tenants, a TRO or a preliminary injunction may be available to keep a particularly abusive landlord off the rented premises, require the landlord to restore wrongfully terminated utilities, or force compliance with the landlord's duty to make repairs. A TRO lasts only a few days, but in an eviction case, it will usually last until the trial date. A preliminary injunction lasts longer, until a court dismisses it or makes the injunction permanent. If a tenant files a lawsuit to force repairs, for example, the actual trial, if there is one, may be scheduled for months away, and the tenant will want to require the landlord to stop the unlawful behavior now while the case is still ongoing.

CHAPTER TEN

HOW DO TENANTS LEAVE?

A tenant who moves without properly terminating a tenancy may be liable for later rent. When one of several co-tenants — roommates or housemates — moves out, that person may even find himself or herself liable to the landlord for damage caused by the remaining co-tenants. This chapter should help avoid those problems. It also should help landlords calculate tenant liability after an early move out or a move without notice. (See also chapter 11.)

1. Ending a Monthly or Weekly Tenancy

Ending a month-to-month or week-to-week tenancy for "no cause" (the termination is not due to misconduct of the landlord or the tenant) is usually quite simple. ORS 90.427 entitles either party to terminate a week-to-week tenancy with 10 days' notice and a month-to-month tenancy (excluding the rental of space for a mobile or floating home; see chapter 13) with 30 days' notice. There are exceptions for certain situations involving military personnel and victims of certain crimes, which are discussed later in this chapter.

In any no-cause situation, the notice must be in writing. It may be served personally or by mail, with three additional days for the mail to arrive. In other words, a 30-day notice starting September 1 could be served personally August 31, but if mailed would have to bear a postmark of August 28 or earlier. The notice should specify the termination date and identify the premises. Sample 26 shows the basic form.

Tenants may give their notice of termination to the person who entered the rental agreement on behalf of the landlord unless they have been informed in writing of the name and address of an owner or other person authorized to manage the premises. It is important to make a copy, and keep it for as long as a landlord is legally able to sue (one year for most claims).

Unless the parties have agreed otherwise, rent is prorated day to day (ORS 90.427(3)). A tenant who is giving 30 days' notice for a date other than the end of a regular rent period can include in his or her notice language similar to this:

> Because this termination date will be 10 days after the next rent payment date, I still owe and will pay one-third of next month's rent, $_____.

SAMPLE 26
TERMINATION NOTICE BY TENANT
(Month-to-month or week-to-week tenancy)

March 27, 20--

Dear J. P. Landlord:

I am currently your tenant at 123 Rental Avenue, Apartment 4. This is my notice that my tenancy will end on April 30, 20--.

Sincerely,

Thomas Tenant

Thomas Tenant

Note: The tenant's no-cause termination notice, if delivered by first-class mail, must provide for three additional days' notice, beyond the 30-day (seven days in a week-to-week tenancy) notice requirement.

Landlords who collect the final month's rent in advance as a deposit must use that prepaid rent for the final month unless the parties have agreed to another use for it (ORS 90.300). A tenant who paid a last month's rent deposit can remind the landlord about this deposit in the notice to terminate:

> As you will recall, I already paid the last month's rent at the beginning of my tenancy.

The tenant who prepaid the last month's rent and decides to terminate shortly after paying the current month's rent, can include the following paragraph in his or her notice:

> As you know, I have already paid the rent for this month, and I paid a last month's rent at the beginning of the tenancy. Because the termination date comes after I've used only one-third of the last month's rent, please return two-thirds $_____ to me now (ORS 90.300(5), ORS 90.427(3)).

ORS 90.300(10) permits double damages if prepaid rent is wrongfully withheld (as in the case of all deposits). Some tenants may feel the need to point this out in their notices. (See chapter 4.)

A tenant who has to leave with less than 30 days' notice should still let the landlord know — in writing — as soon as possible so he or she will have an opportunity to find a new tenant quickly. The current tenant's responsibility for rent liability will continue for a full 30 days after notice only if the landlord makes reasonable efforts to rent the unit but fails to find a new tenant within the 30 days before this tenant's liability ends (ORS 90.125, ORS 90.240, ORS 90.410).

The tenant who has to leave with less than 30 days' notice can try using the following language:

> I realize the termination date in this notice gives you less than 30 days' notice, and I am sorry that I have to give shorter notice. However, please note that unless you make reasonable efforts to re-rent the unit at a fair rental, my liability for rent will terminate as of the date I leave, as stated in ORS 90.410(3).

As a matter of courtesy to the landlord, the departing tenant should inform the landlord of the tenant's availability so the parties can arrange to show the place to prospective tenants. It is also a good idea to review the information regarding the landlord's right of access (see chapter 1, section 3.2).

Tenants should know that once they serve a termination notice, the landlord can use that notice as the basis for an eviction if tenants decide not to move after all. Tenants should weigh carefully the advantages of prompt notice in compliance with the statute against the risks of committing to leave before they are sure about their plans. Of course, the landlord might agree to let the tenants stay, but the landlord has no obligation to do so.

It is unlawful for a landlord to keep a deposit (but not a fee designated for this purpose, in most cases — see special circumstances, section 2.2 below) on the grounds that a tenant failed to stay for a certain length of time. It is arguably not unlawful, however, for a landlord to hold on to cleaning and damage deposits paid by one co-tenant if other tenants remain in the unit after that tenant moves out. The landlord wants to maximize his or her "insurance" against damage to the unit, and, particularly if all the co-tenants have signed one rental agreement together, can argue that there is only one tenancy and that the deposits are due back to the departing co-tenant only when the tenancy of all occupants has terminated and the landlord can assess the damage.

For the departing roommate, getting deposits back can be important — partly because that person will have no control over what happens in the unit after he or she leaves, and partly because it is theoretically possible for the landlord to have that person's money for years before the tenancy officially ends.

When it is time for that tenant to leave, he or she should try to convince the landlord to inspect the unit and determine if any damage has occurred that is chargeable to the tenant. Even if the landlord is unwilling to inspect, the departing tenant should still do the kind of move-out inspection with photos and witnesses recommended in chapter 4 and consider a demand letter and the other remedies listed in that chapter when 31 days have passed without a refund or a damage statement from the landlord.

In the alternative, the departing tenant may want to get the remaining tenants to give him or her money equaling the deposit amount, with the departing tenant giving them and the landlord a written release of liability in return.

For more information on leaving without adequate notice, see the next section.

2. Breaking a Lease

A rental agreement that provides for a tenancy for a specific period of time, such as six months or a year, is a term agreement (a "lease") rather than a month-to-month or week-to-week tenancy. In a typical lease, the tenant cannot terminate the tenancy before the end of the term by simply serving a termination notice appropriate to a month-to-month or week-to-week tenancy. Unless the provisions of the agreement allow for some other right of termination, there must be good cause — related to the tenancy itself — to terminate. Without good cause, the tenant may be liable for the rent for the remainder of the term after the tenant has moved out.

This section explains what qualifies as good cause for tenants to terminate before the term is up, and how to minimize the risks of terminating early without a legal right to do so. The principles involved also apply to terminating month-to-month and week-to-week tenancies with less than the statutory notice.

2.1 What gives a tenant the right to terminate a lease?

ORLTA gives the tenant a right to terminate the tenancy, including a term tenancy, for cause under several circumstances. Perhaps the most important is the right to serve a "fix it or I'm leaving" notice if the landlord violates the rental agreement or the habitability section of the law. This type of termination works only for violations of ORS 90.320 or "material" (serious) violations of the rental agreement. There is no right to terminate if the conditions were caused by the deliberate or negligent acts of the tenant or a guest.

To exercise this right, the tenant must deliver written notice of the problem to the landlord, advising the landlord that the tenancy will terminate unless the problem is corrected. The termination date stated must be at least 30 days from the landlord's receipt of the notice (ORS 90.360). The landlord has 30 days in which to correct the problem unless the complaint is the lack of an essential service, in which case the landlord must correct the problem quickly. (See chapter 6 for the time limits.) To be safe, the tenant should deliver the notice in person. (Mailing the notice adds three extra days to the deadline.) If the landlord fails to cure the problem within the specified time, or if the problem is of a sort that is not "remediable by repairs, the payment of damages, or otherwise," the tenancy ends on the termination date in the notice.

If the landlord fixes the problem, the tenancy does not terminate. So how can this procedure be useful to a tenant who wants to terminate a lease? As a practical matter, a complaint to the landlord seldom results in repairs. In fact, the more strongly worded the tenant's demand for repairs is, the more likely a bad landlord is going to refuse to comply. The failure to repair provides good cause to terminate the lease early.

Sample 27 is an example of a notice designed for a situation that does not involve an essential service. If the tenant wants to use even stronger language in the final paragraph, he or she could try this approach:

> Whether or not you remedy the breaches of your obligations set forth above, I am entitled to damages for the reduction in rental value they have caused to date. I estimate my total damages to date to be $_____. Unless you pay that sum within 10 days, I will pursue my rights under ORS 90.360(2).

There are two limitations on damages of which tenants should be aware. A landlord is liable for noncompliance with the habitability section of the law if the landlord knew or could have been expected to know of the problem that violated ORS 90.320, or when neither the landlord nor the tenant knew or could have been expected to know. If only the tenant knew or should have known and failed to notify the landlord soon enough for the landlord to deal with the problem and prevent the tenant's loss, the landlord has no liability. The other situation in which the landlord is not liable is when the condition was caused by the tenant or someone under the tenant's control.

If an essential service is involved or if the rental has been "posted" by a government agency as unsafe and unlawful to occupy, tenants may be able to impose a shorter time period on the landlord. See chapter 6 for information about the requirements of ORLTA in those situations. Sample 28 covers essential service complaints.

If the landlord actually states that he or she will not remedy the breach, the tenant should be able to terminate effective the date of the notice and move elsewhere — even if the landlord does make repairs, because the tenant acted in reliance on his or her word that no repairs would be made. It's safest to confirm the refusal in writing as shown in Sample 29.

Of course, landlord and tenant both may find it advantageous to agree in writing that the tenant can break the lease in return for releasing the landlord from any liability for the violations that led to the termination. Sample 30 shows one way of doing it.

If the landlord does remedy the breach and the tenant stays, it is possible that the same kind of breach might occur again within six months. In that case, the tenant may terminate by serving a notice at least 14 days (seven days in a week-to-week tenancy) in advance of the termination date without giving the landlord another chance to make repairs.

ORLTA recognizes that some violations cannot be remedied by repairs, the payment of damages, or otherwise. In such a case, the landlord cannot save the tenancy, and a notice something like the one in Sample 31 is appropriate.

In addition to the "fix it or I'm leaving" remedy for essential services and other habitability violations, ORLTA provides tenants with the right to terminate in the following situations:

(a) When the landlord causes a lockout or utility shutoff, the tenant has the immediate right to terminate (ORS 90.375).

(b) When the landlord abuses the right of access, the tenant has the right to give 30 days' written notice of termination (ORS 90.322).

(c) When the landlord threatens eviction, decreases services, or raises rent in retaliation for a tenant's complaints or tenants' union activities, the tenant has the right to give 30 days' written notice (ORS 90.385).

(d) When conditions that aren't the tenant's fault pose a serious and imminent threat to the health or safety of occupants, within six months from the beginning of the tenancy, the tenant has the immediate right to terminate (ORS 90.380(7)).

(e) When a landlord rents a dwelling that a government agency has posted as unsafe and unlawful to occupy, the tenant has the immediate right to terminate (ORS 90.380(2)).

SAMPLE 27
"FIX IT OR I'M LEAVING" NOTICE

March 27, 20--

Dear Mr. J. P. Landlord:

I am your tenant at 123 Rental Avenue, Apartment 4. You are in violation of our rental agreement for failing to supply the paint you promised so I could paint the living room, and the lawn mower you promised so I could maintain the yard. You are also in violation of ORS 90.320 because of these habitability problems:

- Leaking roof
- Three windows missing window panes

If you do not fix these problems by April 30, 20-- *(date at least 30 days after, or 33 days if notice mailed),* our rental agreement will terminate on that date. In addition, I have the right to seek damages for these violations under ORS 90.360.

Thank you for attending to these problems promptly. Please call me at 555-555-5555 to arrange for convenient times to begin the repairs.

Thomas Tenant
Thomas Tenant

Although not all of these grounds for termination expressly require written notice, it is important to use one anyway to make a record of the tenant's position.

The tenant who uses any of these methods to end the tenancy early can sue the landlord for damages in regular court (see chapter 6) or in small claims court (see chapter 4). The damages are the same ones that are available as counterclaims if the landlord sues for unpaid rent as a result of the early termination. If that happens, in addition to the defenses possible in a nonpayment of rent eviction, the tenant may have a claim for failure to refund a deposit (see chapter 4).

"FIX IT OR I'M LEAVING" NOTICE
(Including essential services)

March 27, 20--

Dear J. P. Landlord:

I am your tenant at 123 Rental Avenue, Apartment 4. I write to let you know that you are in violation of ORS 90.320 because of habitability problems at the rental:

- Leaking roof
- Three windows missing window panes
- Broken water heater

Hot water is an essential service. If you do not have the hot water restored within seven days or by April 7, 20-- *[date at least seven days after, or ten days after if notice mailed]*, this tenancy will terminate on April 30, 20-- *[date at least 30 days after this notice or 33 days if notice mailed]*. Even if you fix the water heater within that time, I will terminate the tenancy on April 30, 20-- *[same date as listed for termination date]* if the other habitability problems have not been fixed by that date.

I appreciate your prompt attention to these problems. Please call me at 555-555-5555 to arrange for times to do the needed repairs.

Thomas Tenant

Thomas Tenant

Regardless of which side starts a case after the tenant's early termination, the tenant will not be required to pay rent into court once the tenant is no longer in the unit. In addition, the exercise of a right of termination will be a defense to any rent claimed for a period after the termination date. The former tenant also may have a defense for rent claimed for that time period if the landlord failed to minimize his or her losses. These are discussed below because they are primarily useful to tenants who leave early with no right of termination.

SAMPLE 29
CONFIRMATION OF REFUSAL TO REPAIR

April 5, 20--

Dear Mr. Smith:

This will confirm your statement to me over the phone today that you have no intention of remedying the problems specified in my notice of March 27, 20--. I will rely on your statement and will look for another place to live.

Sincerely,

Thomas Tenant

Thomas Tenant

SAMPLE 30
SETTLEMENT BREAKING LEASE

J. T. Landlord, landlord, and T. R. Tenant, tenant, hereby agree that their dispute concerning the condition of 123 Rental Avenue, Apartment 4 is resolved as follows:

1. Tenant will move out of 123 Rental Avenue, Apartment 4, on or before April 30, 20--, and the tenancy will end as of that date.

2. Landlord hereby releases tenant of any and all liability that might exist concerning the above tenancy.

3. Tenant hereby releases landlord from any and all liability that might exist concerning the above tenancy.

Signed: *J. T. Landlord*
    J. T. Landlord Date: April 5, 20--

Signed: *T. R. Tenant*
    T. R. Tenant Date: April 5, 20--

SAMPLE 31
TERMINATION NOTICE
(Irremedial violation)

March 27, 20--

Dear J. T. Landlord:

I am your tenant at 123 Rental Avenue, Apartment 4. The building inspector has just informed me that the damage you did to the foundation of my house on March 26, 20--, cannot be repaired. Therefore, I hereby give notice, as permitted by ORS 90.360, that our rental agreement will terminate on April 30, 20--. That date is 34 days from today, allowing for me to mail this notice.

Sincerely,

Thomas Tenant

Thomas Tenant

2.2 Special circumstances that permit termination in all kinds of rental agreements

As a policy matter, ORLTA and federal law recognize situations in which holding a tenant to a rental agreement seems especially unfair. Historically, those on active military duty or those called up for service have been protected by the federal Soldiers' and Sailors' Civil Relief Act. In general, that law has protected active-duty military personnel from having court judgments imposed on them without their agreement when they have no way to appear in court to defend against a lawsuit. Landlords who want to evict active service members, even for nonpayment of rent, should get legal advice before doing so.

The 2003 legislature extended similar protections in the case of a rental agreement or a lease for Oregon's National Guard. Guard members can terminate all kinds of rental agreements by showing orders that they are being activated for at least 90 days, and giving written notice of termination. The termination in these cases will be the earlier of 30 days after the next rental payment due date, or the last day of the month after the one-month notice is given. The landlord may not charge any penalty, fee, charge, or loss of deposit. Nor is the landlord entitled to any rent beyond the effective date of the notice.

The 2003 legislature also extended protection from housing discrimination to victims of domestic violence, sexual assault, and stalking crimes. For landlords, this means that some tenants must be permitted to terminate tenancies early so as to protect themselves and their families from the likelihood of future crime. To terminate early, the tenant must give the landlord a minimum of 14 days' written notice specifying the release date, along with verification that the tenant has been the victim of a domestic violence, sexual assault, or stalking crime within the preceding 90 days. The verification can be a copy of a valid court order of protection from such crimes or any other court order restraining a perpetrator from contact with the victim; a copy of a police report about one of these crimes against the tenant or a minor in the household; or a law enforcement officer's written statement that the tenant reported such a crime to the officer.

A tenant who is released from the rental agreement under these circumstances is not liable for rent or damage to the rental after the release date and is not subject to any fee because of the termination of the rental agreement even if the agreement permits fees. If other adults live in the rental unit, they must continue to abide by the rental agreement.

2.3 What if the tenant has no right to terminate?

Even when a tenant must leave before the expiration of a term tenancy, there are still some principles that can help limit liability for further rent. First, a landlord must "mitigate" (minimize) losses. That means he or she must make reasonable efforts to re-rent the premises at a fair rent; otherwise the rental agreement terminates as soon as he or she knows the tenant is gone. Second, the tenant may have the right to sublet or assign the rental agreement, unless the existing rental agreement expressly says the tenant doesn't. Thus, if the current tenant can find a new tenant willing to take over at the same rent and to stay for at least the rest of the term, the current tenant should have no further rent liability unless the landlord has a good reason to reject the new tenant. A notice appropriate for such a situation is shown in Sample 32.

SAMPLE 32
NOTICE OF TERMINATION AFTER FINDING NEW TENANT

March 31, 20--

Dear Mr. J. T. Landlord:

I am currently your tenant at 123 Rental Avenue, Apartment 4. My lease expires December 31, 20--. Unfortunately, I have to break the agreement, as I will be leaving by April 30, 20--. I am sorry to inconvenience you like this.

The law requires you to make reasonable efforts to re-rent the apartment at a fair price or to accept a termination of the rental agreement as of the date you are served notice of my "abandonment" (ORS 90.410). Fortunately, I have located someone who is willing to take over the remaining period of my tenancy at the same rent. His name is Barry Roberts and he can be reached at 444-444-4444. I don't think you will have any reason to reject him as a tenant, unless there is something I don't know about his background that makes him unacceptable. My liability for rent will terminate April 30, 20--, if you do not offer him the tenancy. If you do accept him, my liability will end as of the date his tenancy starts.

Thank you for your cooperation.

Sincerely,

Thomas Tenant

Thomas Tenant

With a sublease, the new tenant would pay rent to the departing tenant, who would still have the legal liability to pay the new person's money to the landlord. With an assignment, the new tenant would pay rent directly to the landlord. In either case, however, the former tenant may be liable to the landlord for any rent the new tenant fails to pay during the rest of the term.

Finding a new tenant is the safest way to leave without a right of termination, but it is essential to explain the situation to the new tenant. The departing tenant who does not do so may end up liable for damages to that new tenant if there is trouble the new person could have avoided by knowing the whole story.

Unfortunately, it may be impossible to find a new tenant on short notice. In such a situation, the departing tenant should offer to make every possible accommodation to the landlord to help him or her find a new tenant. One way to do that is to provide the landlord with a schedule of convenient times to show the rental. It would be possible to replace the last paragraph in Sample 32 with something like this:

> Because we have a mutual interest in finding a new tenant, I will be glad to do everything possible to assist you. I will be happy to be available 9 a.m. to 9 p.m. Saturdays, Sundays, and Wednesdays to show the premises for the next few weeks. Please let me know if you want me to do this.

If you leave early without a right of termination and your landlord sues for unpaid rent, you may have a defense if you can show either that the landlord failed to make reasonable efforts to find a new tenant or that he or she unreasonably rejected a new tenant. Also, you may have the same remedies of recoupment and counterclaim available to a tenant who terminates with a right to do so, plus any of the additional defenses listed earlier in this section.

Of course, you and your landlord may be able to settle your claims against each other, but make sure you do it in writing. (**Note:** If a lawsuit is already pending against you, the case doesn't necessarily "just go away" even if you have a written agreement. You will need court papers showing the case was settled. Legal advice could be quite helpful at this stage.)

ORS 90.410 limits the liability of a tenant who leaves without properly terminating a tenancy or leaves before its termination. The tenant's responsibility for rent ends as soon as the landlord rents the dwelling unit to a new tenant (regardless of the rental amount). There is also no liability to pay rent if the landlord fails to make reasonable efforts to re-rent the dwelling at a fair rent or if the landlord "accepts the abandonment as a surrender." This would occur, for example, if the landlord gave the tenant an eviction notice or otherwise acted as if the tenancy has terminated. In such cases, the rental agreement is considered to be terminated on the date the landlord knew or should have known of the abandonment.

3. Are You Gone Yet?

Tenants should do their best to make sure the landlord is aware that they have moved out and when they have moved out. Not only can this precaution stop their liability for continuing rent, it can also protect them from a claim of damage to the rental caused after they no longer have access to the place.

ORS 90.147 lets the tenant give actual notice to the landlord that the tenant is giving up the unit. Turning in the keys to the unit is a good indicator of this. Returning keys by mail is acceptable, but using the mail gives the landlord three additional days to say the unit is still under the tenant's control. The tenant may want to follow up a "Good-bye! I'm moving out now!" announcement with a confirming letter, keeping a copy, if the tenant's liability for rent is in question. The following sample language could be used in the letter:

> As I mentioned yesterday when I turned in my keys
> to the apartment at 2:00 p.m., I officially moved out
> then.

It is always a good idea to give the landlord a copy of a forwarding address and a contact phone number, too.

A tenant who leaves belongings in the rental or does not return the key or otherwise inform the landlord of his or her departure may be prolonging the time for which the landlord can reasonably charge rent, because the tenant hasn't made it clear that the tenancy is finished (ORS 90.148). Even though a landlord has a duty to find a replacement tenant to minimize any damages from a prior tenant's early move out, the landlord has to be sure the tenant is gone before that duty begins.

CHAPTER ELEVEN

WHAT LANDLORDS CAN DO WITH BELONGINGS LEFT BEHIND; HOW TENANTS CAN GET BELONGINGS BACK

Several county law librarians say that one of the most common questions they receive is, "How can I get a landlord to return my possessions?" It's a question that sometimes comes up during a tenancy and sometimes after one has ended.

For their part, conscientious landlords have struggled with the other side of the issue: What do I do to get my money if the tenant owes me rent? How can I be sure that a tenant has really moved out and discarded his or her belongings? What am I supposed to do with a former tenant's abandoned pet? How can I get rid of a mobile home when the tenant is still paying for it and a bank or other lender is involved? What happens when the person who moved out of a rental on a mobile home space wasn't the owner of the mobile home — who is responsible for it and its contents now? Changes in the law over the past several years have provided answers to these questions, but the questions themselves indicate how complicated the answers can be (ORS 90.425, ORS 90.675).

ORS 90.675 covers abandoned manufactured or floating homes in facilities only; ORS 90.425 covers all other abandoned property, including personal belongings inside a home in a facility and homes not in facilities.

One thing is still very clear: for more than 30 years, it has been unlawful for a residential landlord to seize belongings to make up for rent unpaid by a tenant during or after a tenancy. Nor can a landlord hold tenant belongings as "ransom" to force the tenant to pay rent. A landlord who enters onto the tenant's premises for the purpose of seizing the tenant's belongings for this reason risks statutory damages for unlawful entry and unlawful debt collection (ORS 90.322, ORS 90.420, and ORS 646.608). (See chapter 8.) The tenant may be eligible for twice his or her actual damages (ORS 90.425). In one such case, a court awarded more than $6,000 against a landlord for the "tort of conversion" (i.e., the civil equivalent of theft under criminal law). In addition, the landlord gives up any claims for unpaid rent and for cleaning or repair costs unless they were incurred as a result of the tenant's grossly negligent or deliberate damage to the premises.

Landlords can hold the tenant's belongings in only three instances:

(a) After an eviction judgment if the judgment has not been enforced and the tenant has been continuously absent for at least seven days after the judgment was signed

(b) After an eviction judgment has been enforced by a sheriff and the tenant has been removed by the sheriff

(c) After the tenant permanently left the premises when there is no eviction judgment

Even in these instances, landlords continue to have obligations to former tenants, as described below.

In the first two instances described here, it will be easy for the landlord to determine when he or she has the right to hold or remove the tenant's belongings. Even in these instances, landlords continue to have obligations to former tenants, as described below.

How does a landlord know when a tenant has abandoned or relinquished the rental (situations (c) above)? ORLTA says that the landlord must reasonably conclude under all the circumstances that the tenant does not intend to come back. Believing in good faith that the tenant has been absent for more than a week, the landlord has the right to enter the property without notice to inspect. If the phone and lights are disconnected and the tenant has taken most of his or her belongings away, the tenant's pet is gone, and the key to the rental is on the kitchen table, for example, the landlord should have no trouble convincing a court that it was reasonable to believe the tenant had abandoned the premises and the things inside it. A tenant who is gone for a week to the hospital or on vacation, on the other hand, is not likely to have packed up to move out permanently. A prudent landlord will check with neighbors, the tenant's employer, or others likely to know the tenant's plans.

1. What Landlords Can Do

A landlord who is owed rent by a departing tenant will be tempted to keep the tenant's belongings. As a general rule, however, personal and household belongings are likely to be protected — "exempt" — from being collected to pay off debts. Most creditors, landlords included, have no right to such exempt property, even if they have a court order entitling them to payment. There is a public interest in making sure debtors are not left completely destitute. On the other hand, the landlord should generally be entitled to recover the costs of handling a tenant's abandoned property if doing so won't deprive the tenant of exempt property. How ORLTA allocates the costs is described below.

In the three circumstances described the section above, the landlord must exercise due care to deal with the property for a prescribed period, must give notice to the tenant, and must allow the tenant to reclaim the goods within that period. The notice must be in writing and personally delivered to the tenant, or sent by first-class mail and addressed to the premises, the tenant's forwarding address, if any, and any post office box known to the landlord. Thus if the notice is not delivered in person, it may have to be mailed to three different addresses.

If the property is a recreational vehicle, or mobile home (manufactured dwelling), the landlord must also give a copy of the notice to any lienholder of the mobile home, any owner other than the tenant, and the county tax collector and assessor where the manufactured home or floating home is located. For all but the lienholder, notice must be delivered or mailed first class; for the lienholder, notice must be by certified mail with a return receipt. The notice itself must state whether there is a lienholder of the property.

Recent changes in the law should make it easier for landlords to know whether the tenant or someone else is the actual owner of the mobile or floating home or recreational vehicle, and whether someone else has a financial interest in or a lien on the property. Beginning in 2003, the Oregon Department of Consumer and Business Affairs took on the responsibility of tracking the ownership rights in those kinds of property, and sales of those kinds of property come with new reporting requirements for dealers and lenders.

Before having to deal with the laws governing how to get rid of abandoned property, the landlord must make sure it really is abandoned. That is the purpose of the notice mentioned above: to give the tenant, any other owner, or a lienholder a chance to claim and remove the property. For most kinds of personal property, the landlord's notice must state that the property is considered abandoned and specify a date of disposal no fewer than five days after delivery (eight days if mailed) of the notice. (The time period for recreational vehicles and mobile homes is a minimum of 45 days.) If the tenant or an owner or lienholder responds on or before the date specified in the notice and indicates an intent to reclaim the goods, the landlord may not dispose of the goods until 15 days (30 days for mobile or floating homes or recreational vehicles) after the response or until the date specified in the landlord's notice, whichever is later. During this after-notice period, the law requires that the landlord make the property available for removal "by appointment at reasonable times." The notice must contain this information, as well as how to contact the landlord. The notice must state that all of the property is stored at a place of safekeeping. For recreational vehicles, mobile homes, and floating homes, storage must be at the rental space. The notice must state how the landlord plans to dispose of the property, either by selling it or giving or throwing it away. If the tenant simply left the premises or left after a court ordered an eviction, but before a final lockout by the sheriff, the notice must say whether the landlord requires payment of removal or storage fees before allowing the tenant to take the property. See Sample 33 and Sample 34.

After giving notice, the landlord must store the property in a safe place and exercise reasonable care for the property. The landlord may promptly dispose of rotting food and allow an animal

SAMPLE 33
NOTICE TO TENANT REGARDING ABANDONED PROPERTY

April 15, 20--

To: *([Tenant's name]*
[premises where tenant had been living] and
[any forwarding address known] and
[any post office box known]

The personal belongings you left at 123 Rental Avenue *[premises]* when you moved out appear to be abandoned. If they are not abandoned, you must contact me by April 23, 20-- *[a specific date, no sooner than five days after the date of the notice, or eight days after the date of the notice if mailed]*, to claim them. You can reach me at 777-888-5555 *[phone number or physical address]* to make an appointment for a reasonable date and time to pick up your belongings. Until then, I will store them at a place of safe-keeping.

Because you were removed from the rental by the sheriff after a court-ordered eviction, you do not have to pay any removal or storage costs at the time you collect your things.

[Or, as appropriate:] Because you moved out without the sheriff's having to lock you out of the rental after a court-ordered eviction, I can and will require you to pay the reasonable or actual cost of removing and storing your things as a condition for your being allowed to get them. Those costs are $_____.)

If I do not hear from you by April 23, 20--, or if, after I hear from you and we arrange a date and time for you to pick up your belongings, you do not come to get your things then or arrange another time within 15 days after you contact me, I can dispose of your things or sell them.

[As appropriate:] The law permits me to destroy or give away your things if they reasonably appear to be worth no more than $500. Having examined the items, it is my reasonable belief that they are worth less than $500, and, at the end of the waiting period described above, I will throw them away.

Note: See Sample 34 for a notice including abandoned property such as recreational vehicles, manufactured dwellings, and floating homes.

SAMPLE 34
NOTICE TO TENANT REGARDING ABANDONED PROPERTY INCLUDING RECREATIONAL VEHICLES AND MANUFACTURED OR FLOATING HOMES

April 15, 20--

To *[tenant's name and address of rental, and most recent forwarding address known to landlord, and post office box address known to landlord; or personal delivery to tenant]*

To *[owner of the property, if different from tenant, at any address known to landlord, sent by first-class mail]*

To *[each lienholder at every address known to landlord or of record, by first-class mail, certified and requesting a return receipt]*

To *[the tax collector and assessor in the county where a manufactured home or floating home has been left by the tenant]*

Among the belongings left behind at 123 Rental Avenue *[at address of premises]*, are a recreational vehicle and your mobile home. The time period within which you must contact me to retrieve either or both of these things is 45 days from the date of this notice, May 30, 20-- *[specify date]*. If you do not contact me by that date, or if you contact me and then fail to collect them within 30 days of that contact, I will sell or otherwise dispose of them.

[As appropriate:] According to the tax assessment, the mobile home is worth less than $8,000. Under the law, I can throw it away if you do not claim it and collect it.

[Name] has a lien on the mobile home; therefore he/she/it also has the right to claim and collect it.

control agency or, if that is not possible, a humane society to take abandoned pets or livestock.

If the tenant, owner or lienholder fails to reclaim the goods during the required period, the landlord may sell them by private or public sale. (See ORS 90.425 and ORS 90.675 for a detailed description of how the sale must be conducted.) The landlord may deduct from the sale the costs of notice, storage, and sale, as well as any unpaid rent; the balance (if any) goes to pay county taxes, then to any lienholder, then to the tenant or owner with an accounting. If the tenant or owner cannot, "after due diligence," be found, the net proceeds must be paid to the county treasurer to be held for three years, and will revert to the general fund if unclaimed.

The landlord must take additional steps before selling a recreational vehicle, or mobile or floating home. The landlord must take the following steps:

(a) Arrange for publication in a newspaper of general circulation of a notice of sale twice in consecutive weeks, providing all of the information required by ORS 90.425(10)(a)(B)

(b) Provide written notice to the tenant, and owner or lienholder (if any) prior to the sale

(c) Obtain an affidavit of publication from the newspaper after the second publication

(d) Get written proof from the county that all taxes have been paid or that the county does not object to the sale

The statute also provides a way to get back property taxes waived under certain circumstances.

If the tax-assessed value of a mobile or floating home is $8,000 or less, the landlord can destroy or dispose of it without following these procedures.

The landlord may but does not have to attempt to transfer title and registration of the vehicle or home through the appropriate state agency.

If the landlord reasonably determines that the value of the tenant's other (non-mobile-home or recreational vehicle) goods is $500 or less or so low that the proceeds of any sale would probably not cover the costs of storage and public sale, the landlord may destroy the goods if they are not claimed in the permitted time. The landlord also can donate the goods to nonprofit organizations or nonfamily members.

The landlord is liable to the tenant for any loss arising from the landlord's negligence during storage. If the landlord violates the tenant's rights under the abandoned property section, he or she is liable for twice the tenant's actual damages. On the other hand, a landlord who complies with the statute completely and in good faith will have no liability to a tenant later on for loss or damage to the tenant's personal property.

Mobile homes and floating homes within a facility that appear to be abandoned are dealt with similarly, although there are some significant differences. A careful landlord with an abandoned mobile home, in or out of a facility, will get guidance from a lawyer to ensure compliance with the requirements of this complex law, if only because of the significant value of some mobile homes, and the involvement of lienholders.

Assuming that the tenant claims the abandoned property, the landlord does not have the right to sell the abandoned goods to cover the costs of the eviction action, damages, or other expenses arising from the tenancy, and the tenant cannot be required to pay these charges as the cost of getting the goods back from the landlord.

This doesn't let the tenant off free. The costs of storage and notice can be added to an eviction or other judgment to be enforced later, to the extent that the tenant has any nonexempt assets. The law provides for two other options that can help landlords, tenants, and lienholders deal with manufactured or floating homes left behind. First, a lienholder can make a landlord enter into a 12-month storage agreement under which the landlord will allow the property to remain on site in exchange for a storage fee (the equivalent of rent while the lienholder tries to sell the unit or arranges for its removal. Second, if the mobile home becomes abandoned as the result of the death of the tenant, then a personal representative can make the landlord enter a similar storage agreement for 45 days or the length of probate, whichever is longer.

For all abandoned property, the parties can enter into an agreement up to seven days before — or any time after — the tenant moves away, to waive the requirement for the landlord to follow all the procedures needed to declare the property abandoned. Such an agreement must be entered into in good faith — a landlord cannot require it — and would have to be signed by any lienholders or other owners of the unit before it could be enforced.

2. How Tenants Can Get Their Belongings Back

Tenants faced with moving out should do everything they can to take their belongings with them. If that is not possible, then it is important to have documentation of what is left behind and how much it is likely to be worth. Trying to convince a court of the value of something you can't even prove you own is almost always a losing battle, and dishonest landlords know it. At the very least, the departing tenant should make a list of the belongings and have a reliable friend double-check the list after examining the belongings. (The process is similar to the way to protect security deposits and defend against damage claims described in chapter 4.) In some cases, a tenant may be tempted to disappear without telling the landlord he or she is moving out and leaving things behind. This is not only bad manners, but also not a very smart way to safeguard property the tenant wants to retrieve later: the landlord becomes responsible for keeping the tenant's belongings safe only after the landlord knows or reasonably should know that the tenant has left and left behind the belongings.

When the landlord claims that the tenant abandoned goods, the tenant must act promptly to demonstrate the things have not been abandoned. If the landlord has not yet given or attempted to give the tenant the required written notice described above, the landlord probably is not even entitled to storage costs. Still, the careful tenant should bring a witness and (unless evicted and removed from the home by the sheriff) an amount of money that would be reasonable for storage costs, and ask the landlord for the belongings. If the landlord refuses, he or she is likely to be liable for "conversion" of the tenant's belongings — the civil equivalent of theft under the criminal law.

If the goods are in the custody of a commercial storage company, its charges will have to be paid before it will release anything. Its charges may include the costs of removal. A lawyer may be able to help establish that the goods were never abandoned and may convince the landlord to settle the case by returning the belongings. Otherwise, the tenant will probably have to pay the storage company and seek damages from the landlord in small claims court or, with a lawyer's help, in a civil action in a regular court. The tenant's only other option is to bid for the goods in the sale when the storage company eventually sells the goods to satisfy its storage lien.

Sample 35 is a letter that a tenant might write to claim property after getting a notice of abandoned property from a former landlord. If the tenant did in fact abandon things, he or she would not write in the last sentence in Sample 35. The mere fact that the tenant did not remove all of his or her belongings at once does not prove that he or she abandoned what was left behind. The second date in the response should be either 15 days (30 days for recreational vehicles or mobile or floating homes) from the date on which the tenant gave his or her response to the landlord, or the same date as specified in the landlord's notice, whichever is later. (If you have any trouble, see a lawyer.) **Note:** A tenant who reaches an agreement with the landlord about retrieving property should put the agreement in writing.

SAMPLE 35
RESPONSE TO LANDLORD'S NOTICE
CONCERNING ABANDONED GOODS

June 25, 20--

Dear Mr. J. T. Landlord:

In response to your notice of June 20, 20--, I intend to remove my belongings that you now have no later than July 3, 20--. I did not abandon these things and I do not waive any right I may have against you for your having taken them.

Sincerely,

Thomas Tenant

Thomas Tenant

2.1 A simple court action to get property back

ORS 105.112(2) offers a simple court proceeding for tenants who just want their belongings back from a landlord who has taken the belongings unlawfully. This remedy does not work if the landlord has already destroyed or thrown away the tenant's things. Money damages are not available through this proceeding, but attorney fees are. Form complaints (for tenants) and answers (for landlords) are available in the clerk's office, and the language is designed to guide the parties and the court to a correct analysis of who is entitled to the property.

To use the complaints procedure, the tenant should study the complaint form in ORS 105.112(2)(a) and decide which one applies to his or her situation. If the tenant cannot find a paragraph that applies, he or she is probably not entitled to an order compelling the landlord to return the tenant's belongings. If the tenant does find an applicable one, he or she will go to the clerk's office, pay the filing fees (or ask that the fees be waived or deferred on grounds of indigence as with an eviction answer), check the right paragraph, and fill out the rest of the form.

A landlord who is served with a complaint for return of personal property should study the answer form in ORS 105.112(2)(c). A landlord who cannot find a paragraph that applies to his or her situation probably has no defense. (To keep the case from going to a trial and increasing costs, the landlord should return the tenant's things immediately and negotiate for a stipulated settlement of the case.)

If the facts are unique, the "Other" box should be checked. The forms lay out all of the applicable law. If both parties find paragraphs to check, the issues will be identified for trial.

If the court decides that the property should be returned to the tenant, it may order the sheriff to seize the property and return it to the tenant, or it may give the landlord some time in which to deliver the property to the tenant to avoid further fees. The costs and fees may be added to the judgment in favor of the prevailing party, who may also seek attorney fees if represented by counsel.

CHAPTER TWELVE

FEDERAL HOUSING PROGRAMS

Historically, government-subsidized housing programs have made it possible for some of the lowest-income members of our society — people with disabilities, the elderly, single-parent families — to have decent, affordable housing coupled with protections from arbitrary evictions. At the same time, these programs have made construction and management of subsidized units profitable for private landlords.

In recent years there have been dramatic changes for both tenants and landlords. One result is that, in an area where the law formerly was stable and relatively predictable, now the law is often unclear. Tenants in particular should always seek legal advice if they are threatened with termination of their tenancies.

There continue to be many types of federally supported housing, including government-operated housing, government-subsidized apartment complexes, and rent subsidies that tenants can use in apartments and houses. For most of these types of federal housing, many of the rights of landlords and tenants are codified in constantly changing regulations published first in the Federal Register (FR) and then, with official numbering, in the Code of

Federal Regulations (CFR). The rights of tenants in federally supported housing exist primarily as a result of lawsuits by many tenants who asserted their rights vigorously in cases against the Department of Housing and Urban Development (HUD), in which federal courts found that HUD was violating its duties under federal statutes. As these tenants discovered, not even federal landlords always know or obey the law when compliance is expensive.

The broadest, and most current, source of information about the whole range of federal housing programs is made available online and in publications by the National Housing Law Project:

> 614 Grand Avenue, Suite 320
> Oakland CA 94610
> Telephone: 510-251-9400
> Web site: www.nhlp.org

In general, federal programs have substantial limits on the amount a tenant must pay as rent, they limit in varying degrees the grounds on which a tenant can be evicted, and they may impose additional obligations on participating landlords. All of these limitations may provide a tenant with a defense to an eviction that would be unavailable without federal involvement.

1. Public Housing

Public housing projects are constructed and managed by a "local housing agency" (also known as a housing authority) that must answer to requirements of both state and federal law. Thus, ORLTA applies to housing authorities.

Public housing gives people with incomes below 80 percent of the median income in a particular area an opportunity to rent inexpensive units. Federal law bases the rent amount on a percentage of the tenant's income. Some units are set aside for elderly persons or those with disabilities.

Public housing tenants are entitled to have a written lease listing many of the rights given in ORLTA and, in some cases, adding certain other rights, for example:

(a) Regular redetermination of rent to assure that a tenant will not pay more (or less) than allowed by federal law

(b) Rent abatement (no duty to pay rent) if the housing authority fails to make major repairs under certain circumstances

(c) A grievance hearing before some kinds of evictions (the tenant is allowed to bring a lawyer)

(d) Eviction based only on good cause — although good cause to evict one member of a household can be used to evict the entire household in some cases

All of these rights can help many public housing tenants who are threatened with eviction. For example, many cases get resolved at the grievance level. A tenant who doesn't ask for or is not entitled to a grievance hearing may still contest the eviction action in court.

In any kind of eviction action, a public housing tenant may have one or more of the following defenses:

- The eviction notice did not give a reason for the eviction, stated an improper reason, or did not state the facts justifying the reason (for example, it is not enough to state "violated section 6-B of the lease").

- The eviction notice did not advise the tenant of a right to an informal conference and to a grievance hearing.

- The housing authority did not give the tenant an informal conference or a grievance hearing when the tenant was entitled to one.

In addition, a tenant facing eviction for nonpayment of rent may have these defenses:

- The rent claimed exceeds the permissible maximum under federal law according to the tenant's income.

- The rent claimed was abated because the housing authority refused to make repairs required in the tenant's lease.

In general, if the reason for the eviction doesn't fit those given by ORLTA, it cannot support an eviction unless it constitutes a material (i.e., serious) violation of the tenant's obligations under the lease. The rights and defenses listed above are in addition to those that the tenant has under state law, as discussed in the rest of this book.

Public housing tenants also can have some influence on the way their projects are run. For more information, see chapter 15.

Applicants for public housing are screened according to criteria determined by each housing authority. A housing authority's admission policy cannot automatically deny admission to a particular group or category of otherwise eligible applicants (e.g., families with children born out of wedlock). Under federal law, however, it may be able to deny applicants with records of crimes within the previous five years; people with active alcohol or drug abuse problems; people who have been evicted from privately owned rentals for good cause in some cases; or some categories of noncitizens. In addition, housing authorities don't always set aside units for the most financially needy. As a result, people poor enough to qualify can be turned away for being "too poor."

An applicant who is denied eligibility for public housing is entitled to be told and to be offered an informal hearing on the denial. Applicants should be aware that, although the hearing may be informal, it is still important. They may bring an attorney to the hearing — and they should, if they can.

Projects with units set aside for elders or people with disabilities must permit pets, although the projects can make reasonable rules about the size, number, and type of pet. They also can require a reasonable amount of pet insurance.

2. Subsidized Housing

Subsidized housing includes multifamily, low-rent housing usually in the hands of private owners who get a federal subsidy to build or pay for the complex and/or payments supplementing the rent paid by tenants. The projects may be funded and overseen by HUD or by Rural Development (RD); a federal agency dedicated to rural housing. The federal government also offers tax credits to some kinds of low-income housing owners. These owners are subject to federal regulations, too.

Like public housing authorities, owners of subsidized projects have obligations under federal law and under their contracts. Local projects can be found by contacting the nearest area office of HUD or RD, listed in the phone book under "US Government."

Although subsidized housing tenants don't have the full range of rights enjoyed by public housing tenants, some have the right at least to an informal procedure before having to face a court. Most are entitled to detailed eviction notices and limits on the landlord's ability to evict them without good cause — rights similar to those of public housing tenants.

Tenants in subsidized housing enjoy all the rights and defenses of private tenants. In addition, they often have defenses to eviction if their subsidized landlord fails to comply with procedural or substantive provisions of federal law. In projects subsidized with funds from the federal HOME fund, federal law gives tenants the right to a full 30-day notice for cause regardless of the kind of cause alleged in an eviction notice. (If the notice offers the tenant a chance to fix the problem to avoid eviction, the time to fix the problem only has to be as long as state law requires, for example, 10 days for a pet violation or 72 hours for unpaid rent.) The subsidizing agency or the tax records office in the county where the complex is located should have information as to whether HOME funds are a part of the subsidy in a particular complex.

Finally, there is also great potential for organized subsidized housing tenants to have some control over the management of their projects.

3. Rent Subsidies for Tenant-Selected Housing

Low-income tenants can sometimes obtain "housing choice vouchers" that will allow the tenants to rent from private landlords — not only apartments but also houses and even shared housing. The tenant pays a limited rent calculated on the basis of income, and the federal government makes up the difference. However, private landlords are not required to accept tenants who want to use vouchers. Landlords of low-income housing tax credit units must accept tenants who have vouchers.

The voucher program is administered by public housing authorities in areas that have such an authority; otherwise the program is administered directly by HUD.

The program is popular with some landlords, who are able to rent to low-income disabled and elderly persons who, without a subsidy, would not be able to live in these rentals. In addition, the monthly subsidy is usually the largest portion of the rent, so if a tenant becomes unable to pay his or her portion, the landlord is not left without any income from the unit while resolving the problem with the tenant.

To qualify for a housing voucher, a tenant's family income must not exceed 80 percent of the median for the locality. The family must apply to a local housing authority or to HUD. Applicants cannot have a recent criminal history or be dependent on alcohol or illegal drugs.

An applicant who qualifies for a voucher likely will spend a considerable amount of time on a waiting list to receive a voucher; a waiting period from six months to two years is unfortunately not uncommon.

The dwelling the tenant wants to rent has to qualify for the voucher program, too. It must have enough space for the applicant family, and it must comply with applicable federal regulations about safety and decency, similar to Oregon's habitability statute. Finally, the total rent — the tenant's share and the subsidy together — must be within the limits established by the HUD schedule for the area.

If a voucher-subsidized housing landlord wants to evict a tenant, it must follow both the requirements of ORLTA and the written rental agreement. If the landlord successfully evicts the tenant using a no-cause notice, the tenant can keep the voucher for use in another rental (within certain time limits that the housing authority requires). However, if the eviction is for cause, the housing authority may decide to terminate the voucher. Tenants have the right to an informal hearing with the housing authority in such a case. It is important to get legal help for such a hearing; although it may be informal, the outcome can have a big impact on the tenant's ability to get decent housing again.

Some housing authorities and helping agencies offer "second chance" programs for tenants who have been evicted for cause by either private or government landlords. Tenants who complete the educational program may become eligible for a voucher or for other subsidized housing.

4. Agency Practices That Are Unfair to Tenants

Applicants and tenants in any kind of government-subsidized housing program should be alert to unlawful practices that may hurt their chances to get into or stay in subsidized housing. Beware of the following problems:

- A housing authority puts a voucher-holding tenant on probation, saying it will terminate the tenant's voucher if the tenant does something wrong in the future. The housing authority does not have the power to do this.

- An agency landlord should not abuse its discretion by evicting one tenant but only warning another tenant about the same conduct.

- Agency-drafted rental agreements should be written in language that non-lawyers can understand.

- When a tenant entitled to an agency hearing asks for a hearing too late, the agency must look at the evidence to see if the tenant had a good reason for the delay.

- Low-income tax credit housing complexes and housing that uses HOME grant funding must provide for good-cause eviction.

- Some housing projects do not follow federal regulations when they increase rents. They may increase the rent too soon and/or too much.

- Agencies sometimes do not make special efforts to recruit Hispanic and Native American populations.

- Families, all of whose members are younger than 18 years old, should not be considered ineligible for agency-subsidized housing because of their age.

- Victims of domestic violence should not be evicted from subsidized housing on the basis that they are crime victims.

- Some subsidized complexes do not provide grievance hearings, thus violating their own rental agreements.

- Some agencies and subsidized landlords define "family unit" to exclude unmarried persons, which is in violation of state law.

CHAPTER THIRTEEN

MOBILE HOME, MANUFACTURED HOME, AND FLOATING HOME TENANCIES

ORLTA has special provisions for mobile home and floating home tenancies. Landlords and tenants should expect some significant differences in the rental rules between general residential tenancies and mobile and floating home tenancies. The special provisions cover the rent of an individual space as well as the rent of space located in "facilities," as discussed in detail below. They generally do not apply to rentals of the dwelling units themselves. In some cases, they may apply to trailers or recreational vehicles: Oregonians whose homes are also their transportation need to know whether their particular housing qualifies for protection under ORLTA. Special provisions also apply to the way manufactured homes can be removed from rental space or disposed of by landlords after the space renter has moved away. Much of the law relating to manufactured housing facilities is contained in ORS 90.505 – 90.840. Some of the information, including important definitions, is in the general sections of ORLTA.

To qualify as a home protected under any of the special provisions of ORLTA, a manufactured dwelling must be —

- a residential trailer constructed before 1962 for movement on the public highways, with sleeping, cooking, and plumbing facilities, intended for human occupancy, and used as a residence;

- a mobile home constructed between January 1, 1962, and June 15, 1976, in accordance with Oregon mobile home law in effect at the time of construction; or

- a manufactured home constructed in accordance with federal manufactured housing construction and safety standards in effect at the time of its construction.

What is a facility? According to ORLTA, a manufactured dwelling facility is a place where there are four or more manufactured dwellings and whose primary purpose is to provide rental space for a fee. (This definition does not include lots in a subdivision with only one manufactured home per lot [ORS 446.003].) A floating home facility is a minimum of four adjacent spaces in the hands of a single owner, again providing space rent for a fee (ORS 90.100).

Mobile or floating home owners who rent space on land (or moorage space on water) that is not a facility are subject to the provisions of ORLTA that apply to regular non-facility tenancies, such as houses and apartments. There are two exceptions to this general rule. First, a landlord who leases only space to the tenant is not responsible for repairing interior electrical or heating problems, repairing a leaking roof, or fixing any other habitability problem in the living unit itself unless the landlord's conduct caused the problem (ORS 90.320). Second, a landlord who wants to evict a space-renting tenant without good cause must give the tenant a minimum of 180 days' notice, not just 30 days (ORS 90.429). All other grounds to evict are the same as those in ordinary residential tenancies.

1. The Rental Agreement

A home-owning renter of space outside a facility may have an oral or written rental agreement with the landlord. Mobile and floating home tenants in facilities, however, are entitled to a written rental agreement that specifies the following:

(a) The location and size of the rented space

(b) Whether the facility is "older person housing" under the federal Fair Housing Act (see chapter 14)

(c) The rent per month

(d) All personal property, services, and facilities to be provided by the landlord

(e) All rules and regulations which, if violated, may be cause for eviction

(f) All refundable deposits, nonrefundable fees, and installation charges imposed by the landlord or governmental agencies

(g) Improvements that the tenant may or must make to the rental space, including plant materials and landscaping, and what happens to them at the end of the tenancy

(h) Any limitations the landlord applies in approving a purchaser of a mobile home as a tenant in the event the tenant elects to sell the mobile home (including but not limited to pets, number of occupants, credit references, character references, and criminal records)

(i) Any restrictions against the tenant's selling his or her home to someone who intends to leave the home on the rental space (i.e., the landlord may wish to approve the purchaser as a tenant)

(j) The length (term) of the tenancy

(k) How the rental agreement or rules can be changed

(l) How the landlord and the tenant are to give each other legally required notices.

A rental agreement may contain other provisions as well, including a requirement that the tenant pay directly to the landlord any utility or service fees that are billed by the provider directly to the landlord. The landlord cannot claim more than the cost of the service or utility.

2. Statement of Policy

Before entering into a rental agreement, the prospective tenant must be shown a copy of the facility's general policy. The policy includes many of the same provisions the rental agreement is required to contain. It must also set out three other important procedures:

(a) How the facility will treat terminations of rental agreements (e.g., automatic renewal, automatic eviction, or something in between — an extremely important consideration for the tenant who may be faced with moving a $40,000 home!)

(b) How the facility will handle closure or sale of the facility

(c) Which informal dispute resolution procedures the facility uses

The landlord must provide a one-page summary of information about any tenants' association, written by the association. The landlord must also provide its policy about the removal of a manufactured dwelling, including a statement that the removal policy may affect the value of the unit when the tenant tries to sell it.

The tenant is entitled to a copy of the policy at the time of signing and entering into the rental agreement. The tenant also is entitled to a copy of any facility rules.

Facility residents usually have a large financial investment in their homes. The homes cannot be moved without great expense and risk. These facts make facility tenants particularly vulnerable to abuse by unscrupulous landlords. Disputes between the parties are common. Recognizing the difficulties of this living situation, the state's Housing and Community Services Department began in 1989 to help mobile home facilities establish an informal dispute resolution process and facilitate discussion among the parties. This work is the responsibility of the department's office of community relations. Unfortunately, the scope of its role is unclear. The law requires it only to "undertake, participate in, or cooperate with persons and agencies in such conferences, inquiries, meetings, or studies as might lead to improvements in mobile home and manufactured dwelling park landlord and tenant relationships"; maintain information about facilities — location, number of spaces, etc.; and refer disputants to mediation, arbitration, and other dispute resolution resources (ORS 446.453).

It is the landlord who determines which dispute resolution process the facility will use. In one case that showcased a landlord's bad faith, the process was "contact my lawyer." Even when good faith is not at issue, tenants need to know how the landlord's choice affects their rights. Mediation may be offered by the office of community relations or it may be available at no charge through a community mediation service. Not every community has such a service, and communities that do may not handle these kinds of problems. Thus, tenants may be looking at paying for mediation service.

Furthermore, agreements reached in mediation are not binding; the discussion leading up to an agreement cannot be disclosed in court (ORS 90.771). Arbitration, on the other hand, can be binding and expensive. If the arbitrator's ruling does not satisfy one of the parties, the ability to appeal the decision is quite limited. Oregon's eviction law does provide that, if asked, a court must abate an eviction case to allow arbitration if it is required by the rental agreement, but the arbitration cannot cause a delay in the case of more than 30 days without the parties' agreement (ORS 105.138).

3. Rules of the Facility

The law requires facilities to provide written rules so tenants will know what kind of conduct can jeopardize their tenancies. By law, any rules a facility adopts must be clear and reasonably related to the landlord's intent to promote the safety, convenience, or welfare of the tenants; to distribute services and facilities fairly; and to preserve the landlord's property from abuse. They must not be designed to relieve the landlord of his or her duties toward the tenants. A rule that does not meet these requirements is not enforceable. However, facility rules and regulations do not have to be identical for all tenants at all times (ORS 90.510). Rules and rule changes are discussed in more detail later in this chapter.

No facility rental agreement or rule is allowed to infringe on the right of the tenants or tenants' association to meet peaceably at reasonable times in common areas or recreational areas of the facility (ORS 90.750). What constitutes reasonable times includes at least from 8 a.m. to 10 p.m. daily. The landlord may charge a reasonable deposit for the use of common areas or recreation areas by tenants so long as the terms of the deposit are in writing. The landlord cannot require tenants to get a bond or insurance as a condition of using those areas.

Facility landlords have the general authority to establish occupancy guidelines. These must not be more restrictive than to limit occupancy to two persons for each bedroom and they must be based on reasonable factors. A facility landlord may, but need not, consider the list of statutory "reasonable" considerations and is expressly authorized to consider "limitations placed on utility services governed by a permit for water or sewage disposal." Intended to provide some protection against liability for discrimination under the Fair Housing Act, these statutes are of doubtful benefit to landlords. (For more about the Fair Housing Act, see chapter 14.)

What happens if either the rental agreement or the statement of policy omits a provision "required" by statute? The short answer is, it depends. For example, if a landlord fails to include in a rental agreement the conditions to be applied to screen a purchaser who wants to become a tenant, it probably means the landlord can't impose conditions at all (ORS 90.680(5)). Failure to mention the process by which notices shall be given means that the parties must fall back on the notice provisions of ORLTA in ORS 90.150 and ORS 90.155. Relying on those provisions means, among other things, that someone previously authorized to receive notices and demands on the landlord's behalf is stuck with that role until the landlord notifies the tenant otherwise in writing (ORS 90.605). Whether a landlord's failure to mention the rule change process in the rental agreement or rent adjustment policy in the statement of policy prevents the landlord from making rule changes or raising the rent remains an open question.

What is certain is that the rental agreement cannot diminish the parties' rights to notice and the manner of counting days (ORS 90.160).

4. Conditions of Occupancy

No facility landlord may impose conditions of rental or occupancy that unreasonably restrict the tenant or prospective tenant in his or her choice of mobile or floating home dealers, fuel suppliers, furnishings, goods, services, or accessories. A landlord may not give preference to a tenant who purchased a mobile or floating home from a particular dealer, and a dealer cannot require a purchaser to rent space at a particular facility or group of facilities (ORS 90.525).

Nonetheless, a facility landlord can impose a requirement on prospective tenants to make certain kinds of improvements, such as fences, landscaping, or outbuildings. To do so lawfully, the landlord must provide a written disclosure to every prospective tenant before the person signs a rental agreement, of the improvements the facility will require. This disclosure must specify the type and size of structures and other improvements, materials and finishing, site preparation requirements, installation charges to be imposed by the landlord and government agencies, identification of improvements to be left onsite when the tenant moves, and system development charges to be paid by the tenant (ORS 90.514). The disclosure is to be made on a model form designed by the attorney general's office (ORS 90.516).

5. Termination

Tenants in facilities may terminate their tenancies with or without cause, just as in other kinds of tenancies. A tenant may terminate a manufactured or floating home agreement — month-to-month or fixed-term — without cause by giving at least 30 days' written notice to the landlord. The notice must state the termination date. The landlord cannot require longer advance notice (ORS 90.620). A tenant who is a victim of domestic violence may be able to terminate sooner. (See chapter 10.)

A tenant who decides to terminate for cause can do so under several circumstances. In most of them, the for-cause notice must give the landlord an opportunity to fix the problem, thereby keeping the tenancy from terminating for that cause. A tenant can terminate on short notice when the tenant is unable to obtain utilities and services that were supposed to be available under the rental agreement. (See ORS 90.315 and chapter 6.) Under ORS 90.360, the tenant can terminate if the landlord does not provide essential services or perform other duties so as to be materially out of compliance with the rental agreement or habitability requirements under ORS 90.730. Depending on the severity and type of problem, the landlord may have only a very short time in which to remedy the problem. The same is true for lockouts and unlawful utility shutoffs, or renting in violation of health and safety codes (ORS 90.375, ORS 90.380). (See chapter 6 for specific time limits and restrictions.)

As a practical matter, hardly any tenant will want to spend what may be thousands of dollars to remove his or her home from the facility in the hope of finding another one, a reality that means for-cause "fix it or I'm leaving" terminations by tenants acting alone are rare. The tenant who feels compelled to move because of landlord misconduct or neglect may be better off gathering evidence for a damage claim or for injunctive relief or both. The conditions that would make a facility tenant think about terminating for cause are likely to be problems for other tenants as well; tenants may want to form a union to effect change. (See chapter 15 for information and resources.)

Because of the increased risks to facility space renters who are forced to move, the law provides for these tenants some protections that tenants in ordinary rental housing do not have. For example, a tenant with a month-to-month rental agreement in a facility can be evicted only for cause. A landlord who wants the right to evict without cause must enter into a fixed-term agreement of no shorter than two years (ORS 90.540). If this landlord wants to continue to have the right to no-cause termination, he or she must offer the tenant a new fixed-term agreement at least 60 days before the end of the current term. If the landlord does not do so, the rental agreement converts to a month-to-month rental agreement terminable only for good cause. If a tenant must move as the result of the end of a fixed term lease, the tenant has the right to six months' onsite storage once the tenant has moved so long as the landlord does not have to file an eviction case.

A landlord may terminate a manufactured or floating home space rental prior to the designated termination date in the agreement only for cause (ORS 90.630). Under ORLTA, landlords have several reasons they can use to support a for-cause eviction:

(a) If the tenant violates a law or ordinance that relates to the tenant's conduct as a tenant, or if the tenant violates a valid rule, the landlord may serve a written notice specifying a termination date at least 30 days from the service of the notice and giving the tenant 30 days in which to fix the problem. The "tenant's conduct as a tenant" means failing to perform basic tenant duties. Those duties include keeping the premises free from accumulated trash; proper disposal of infectious waste; use of the premises for their intended purpose; conduct of tenant and tenant's visitors that does not unduly disturb others or cause damage; taking precautions against fire, including maintaining working smoke detectors; and maintaining landscaping (ORS 90.740).

If termination is based on violation of a rule, the violation must be of a rule specified in the rental agreement as one whose violation is a cause for eviction. In any event, the notice must set forth facts sufficient to notify the tenant of the reasons for termination. The tenant can avoid termination by curing the violation within the 30-day period. However, if the violation recurs within six months, the landlord may terminate by serving at least 20 days' written notice specifying the violation and the termination date (ORS 90.630). The prudent landlord will retain a copy of the first notice in the event of a repeat violation; the first notice is a necessary precursor to the second and will have to be produced at an eviction trial.

(b) A landlord can give a minimum of 30 days' written notice of termination to a tenant who does not make repairs to the tenant's home if it is deteriorated or in disrepair (ORS 90.632). The notice in this case must state the problem specifically, and tell the tenant what will correct the problem. The notice must also inform the tenant that he or she can notify the landlord when the correction is complete, and how to notify the landlord for that purpose. If the tenant does not make satisfactory repairs within the time allotted, he or she may be evicted. On eviction, the tenant is obliged to remove the manufactured home. It cannot be sold on site or rented to another person. The landlord may not issue a terminate-and-remove notice based only on the age, style, size, or construction of the manufactured home.

There are conditions under which the tenant can get additional time to complete the repairs, such as if weather conditions would make the repair impossible or ineffective, or if repairs are so extensive they cannot reasonably be completed within 30 days. In these situations, the tenant is entitled to at least 60 additional days to effect the repair. If the condition prompting the notice existed for a year or more with the landlord's knowledge, the tenant is entitled to an additional six months to correct the problem. The tenant must request an extension of time in writing, and before the end of the notice period. An extension is not available if the problem presents a risk of "imminent and serious harm" to people or units in the facility.

Why would the tenant want to give written notice of correction of the problem? There are two practical answers. The first reason is that written notice to the landlord lets the landlord know he or she can now inspect and decide whether the tenant has complied with the notice. If the tenant has not, the landlord can give the tenant further written direction about what needs to be done. (The landlord cannot set up new conditions for the tenant to meet.) The tenant may still have time to do those things to avoid termination. The second reason is that the notice of correction can sometimes be used to stop an eviction. If the tenant's notice of correction is given at least 14 days before the end of the termination period or the extension period and if the landlord doesn't respond in writing about whether the problem is fixed to the landlord's satisfaction, the landlord cannot evict the tenant by claiming the tenant did not correct the problem described in the landlord's termination notice.

(c) A facility landlord who wants to close the facility or a part of it which includes a mobile or floating home space and convert the land or moorage to another use may terminate the rental agreement by giving the tenant at least 365 days' notice in writing. The landlord may terminate on 180 days' notice for the same reason if the landlord finds a space acceptable to the tenant to which the tenant can move the mobile home, and if the landlord pays the cost of moving and setup expenses not exceeding $3,500 (ORS 90.360). In practice, this probably means that a landlord is free to make a deal with a tenant who is willing to accept cash to move more quickly. If the tenant agrees to move sooner than 365 days (or 180 days), the agreement is legal (so long as the right to extended notice wasn't waived in advance).

A landlord may not increase rent to offset payments made to get a tenant to move more quickly, and a landlord may not increase the rent for any reason after giving a facility-closure notice under this section. This limitation applies only to landlords and not to any government agency that takes over the land under its power of eminent domain.

(d) A facility landlord can terminate the rental agreement for repeated late payment of rent. This option is available only after the tenant has paid rent after the grace period three times in the last 12 months, and then only after receiving nonpayment eviction notices. To be able to use this type of termination, in at least the last two of those notices, the landlord must have included a warning to the tenant about the effect of repeated late payment. The actual notice of termination based on repeated late rent payment must be a written 30-day notice stating the reason for the termination. The tenant has no opportunity to cure the problem (ORS 90.630).

(e) If the tenant fails to pay the rent, or the landlord has other cause to evict under ORLTA, the landlord may use the same procedures available to all landlords under that law and the eviction statutes. (See chapter 8.)

6. Rent Increases

As noted above, a facility space rental agreement must be in writing and it must specify the amount of rent. A landlord cannot increase the rent in a lease agreement unless the written rental agreement permits the landlord to do so. Accordingly, a facility landlord who uses a term lease must provide for rent increases in the rental agreement to be sure he or she has the power to raise rent at all during the tenancy. A tenant who wants to be free of all doubt might ask for a provision specifying that rent will not be increased during the tenancy. In either event, the result might well be a formula permitting rent increases only to cover the landlord's increases in taxes and operating expenses.

Landlords who offer month-to-month tenancies must give 90 days' advance written notice of a rent increase. The notice must state the amount of the increase, the total new rent amount, and the date on which the new rate will become effective (ORS 90.600).

Unless the rental agreement provides otherwise, a facility landlord may bill separately for utility service fees and charges assessed by the utility for services to or for spaces in the facility. These charges and fees are not considered part of the rent and so are not subject to the rent increase notice provisions.

7. Retaliation

Mobile home and floating home owners living in facilities have somewhat broader protections from landlord retaliation than do tenants in conventional housing. In addition to the prohibitions of the general retaliation statute, a mobile or floating home landlord may not retaliate by increasing rent, decreasing services, or by bringing or threatening to bring an action for possession after the tenant has —

(a) expressed an intention to complain to a code enforcement agency;

(b) made any complaint to the landlord in good faith;

(c) filed or expressed an intention to file a complaint alleging unlawful discrimination with the Civil Rights Division of the Bureau of Labor and Industries;

(d) performed or expressed intent to perform any other act for the purpose of asserting; protecting, or invoking the protection of any right secured to tenants under any federal, state, or local law;

(e) organized or participated in a tenants' union; or

(f) placed a political sign on or in the tenant's manufactured dwelling, so long as the sign complies with valid placement, size, and "character" restrictions. (The last of these limitations is probably unconstitutional, but the issue has not yet come before a court.) (ORS 90.750, ORS 90.755, ORS 90. 765)

A facility tenant who can show retaliation for any of the points in (a) through (e) above has a claim against the landlord for actual damages or $200, whichever is larger (ORS 90.710). The tenant also has a defense against an attempted retaliatory eviction.

8. Sales of Mobile Homes

A landlord cannot limit a tenant's right to sell a mobile home or forbid a tenant to place a "for sale" sign on or in the mobile home (within reasonable regulations). The landlord may require not more than 10 days' written notice before a sale and a written application from the buyer if the buyer wants to keep the mobile home on the rented space and become a tenant. The landlord may prohibit the prospective purchaser from moving into the dwelling unit until the person has been accepted as a tenant, and can require the current renter of the space to give the prospective purchaser, any lienholders, or any dealers notice of the prohibition and a copy of the facility rules. The landlord may reject the buyer as a tenant only for a reason specified in the written rental agreement. The landlord must furnish both the buyer and the seller with a written statement of the reasons for any rejection. However, a rejection based on a consumer credit report cannot disclose to the seller the contents of the credit report.

If the landlord accepts the tenant as a purchaser, the landlord must inform the purchaser at that time what conditions will be applied if the purchaser later sells the mobile home. These conditions need not be the same as those reserved in the seller's lease, although they must be part of the buyer's rental agreement to be enforceable.

This provision for gradual change is intentional; it balances the right of a tenant moving into a facility to rely on the conditions disclosed at that time in selling the mobile home to a new tenant against the needs of management to make changes over time.

If the buyer wants to become a tenant at the facility, the landlord has a duty to decide quickly whether to accept him or her. The landlord cannot unreasonably reject a prospective purchaser as a tenant. In most cases, the landlord has 7 days to decide, or 10 days if the seller has given the landlord less than 10 days' notice of the sale. The purchaser and the landlord can agree to a longer time if it is needed to complete screening the prospective tenant. If the landlord doesn't require an application, or doesn't act within the time limit —

- the landlord cannot recover damages based on the selling tenant's breach of the landlord's right to screen buyers as tenants;

- the buyer can occupy as a tenant under the same conditions and terms as applied to the seller; and

- the landlord cannot impose terms or conditions that are inconsistent with those applicable to the old tenant without the written consent of the buyer (ORS 90.680).

Note that a buyer has a claim against the seller for damages or $100, whichever is greater, if the seller sells the home before the landlord has accepted the buyer as a new tenant or if the landlord rejects the buyer as a tenant and the seller knew the buyer wanted to stay on as a tenant.

9. Political Rights

Primarily as a result of disputes over tenant organizing rights, several laws have been adopted over the years to protect the political rights of tenants in mobile home or floating home facilities. Essentially, these provisions echo constitutional rights to free speech and assembly, subject to reasonable regulation concerning time, place, and manner. Tenants are permitted to use common areas for meetings, go door-to-door to talk to other tenants, and invite tenant association representatives, public officials, and candidates for office to speak. A landlord need not permit solicitation of money (except by a tenants' association member seeking payment of delinquent dues from another existing member) and may enforce a tenant's request not to be canvassed.

10. Facility Purchase by Associations and Nonprofits

Tenants who wish to buy their mobile home facility can do so by forming a facility purchase association or a nonprofit corporation. This group can get assistance from the state Housing and Community Services Department. The law also gives a duly constituted tenants' association the right to demand notice and good faith negotiation from a facility owner who is attempting to sell a mobile home facility. To be entitled to this procedure, the association must be organized as a corporation or association under the appropriate state statutes, so this is not a last minute project. Once the association receives notice of the proposed sale, it must act very quickly to enforce its right to be considered as a purchaser; the statutes give specific timelines. An association that follows the statutes correctly will have the right to be treated like any other potential buyer, plus the potential for technical and financial assistance from the Housing and Community Services Department. The condominium statutes make it possible for tenants to form a condominium association to try to get financing to buy a facility.

11. When a Tenant Dies

Several interests collide when a facility tenant who has been living alone dies. The facility wants to collect rent for the space and may also want to get rid of an older mobile home as part of an ongoing "upgrade" of the facility. The tenant's heirs, on the other hand, must dispose of the assets of the estate, a process that takes time. In addition, the tenant's home may be subject to a mortgage, property taxes, or other claims by creditors.

A landlord faced with this problem must follow the provisions of ORS 90.675, the abandoned property statute discussed in chapter 11, with a few important differences. If a court has appointed a personal representative for the deceased tenant's estate, or if a will has named a representative, or if the landlord obtained a written designation by the tenant of someone to notify in case of his or her death, the landlord must give the notice of abandoned property to —

(a) the deceased tenant, at the rented space, by first-class mail;

(b) the personal representative of the tenant, personally or by first-class mail; or

(c) any person designated by the tenant for this purpose, personally or by first-class mail.

The notice must state, among other things, that —

(a) the home is considered abandoned;

(b) to claim the property, the representative or designee has until a specified date at least 45 days past the mailing or delivery date of the notice to contact the landlord at an address or phone number contained in the notice;

(c) the property is being stored on the rental space; and

(d) the landlord will make the property available for removal by appointment at reasonable times.

If an heir, or a representative or designee contacts the landlord within the 45-day period, the parties can make a written agreement for storage of the home on site for up to 90 days or the close of probate of the estate, whichever is later. No one may live in the home during the storage period. However, the deceased tenant's representative may sell the home to someone acceptable to the landlord as a tenant (ORS 90.680).

12. Statutory Damages

As mentioned earlier in this book, various provisions of ORLTA carry statutory damages designed to assure a tenant of recovering at least a minimum amount if the tenant goes to court to enforce a right. The facility provisions of the law also carry statutory damages for some violations. A tenant is entitled to at least $200 for a violation of any of the following mobile home protections:

- Freedom from retaliation

- Good cause for evictions

- Valid limits on the sale of a mobile home

- Valid limits on conditions of occupancy

A tenant whose landlord has violated the right to a written rental agreement (and to a copy) has a claim for $100 or actual damages, whichever is greater (ORS 90.710). The landlord can reduce the risk of this violation in two ways:

(a) Within ten days of the tenant's request, the landlord can offer to enter into a written rental agreement consistent with ORLTA and not substantially different from the existing oral agreement.

(b) The landlord can avoid all further liability to all other tenants by offering to enter into written rental agreements with each of the other tenants within 10 days of being served with a complaint (the first paper filed to start a lawsuit) by the first tenant, provided that the offered written agreement is consistent with ORLTA and not a substantial modification of the original bargain.

A buyer of a mobile home is entitled to recover damages of at least $100 from a seller if the sale is made before the landlord approved the buyer as a tenant or if the landlord rejects the buyer, and the seller knew the buyer wanted to stay.

In common with all tenants, a facility tenant who sues successfully for damages is entitled to recover court costs and attorney fees at the trial level and on appeal (if any), in addition to any statutory damages.

13. Rule Changes and Informal Dispute Resolution

A facility landlord may change a rule or regulation — even if the change makes a substantial change in the tenants' bargain — by giving notice as provided in ORS 90.610 that the rule will go into effect no fewer than 60 days after the notice is served, unless tenants of 51 percent of the "eligible" rented spaces in the facility object in writing within 30 days of receiving the notice. The landlord may not change a provision of the rental agreement itself using this method. To be eligible to vote, a tenant must not already be subject to the rule being proposed.

The statute contains the notice form the landlord must use to announce a rule change. The notice must —

- include the language of the existing rule and the proposed changed language;

- specify the number of rented spaces in the facility as of the date of the notice, the last day for written objection, and the date on which the proposed change will become effective if there is no objection; and

- state that the parties may attempt to resolve any differences by using the facility's informal dispute resolution process.

Unless tenants from 51 percent of the facility spaces object in writing to the new rule, it will become part of the agreement. One tenant per space is eligible to vote where the proposed rule is not already in effect. If a tenant objects more than once and in more than one way (e.g., by signing a petition and then writing an objection to the landlord), the most recent objection is the one that counts. A tenant may vote by proxy only if the tenant has a disability that prevents him or her from making the objection in person. Unless the parties agree to some other outcome, the new rule will become effective on the date specified in the notice.

Facility landlords may not change rules or regulations in such a way that a tenant who had a pet legally before notice of the rule change would have to get rid of it. The law provides, moreover, that the tenant can replace that pet with a similar pet. On the other hand, these "grandfathered" pets are subject to any rules or regulations, including new or changed rules and regulations, that apply to all pets in the facility. In rental agreements entered into after October 31, 1997, facility landlords may not charge tenants either a one-time or periodic fee for having a pet; for their part, tenants must sign a pet agreement and provide proof of liability insurance, naming the landlord as a co-insured so he or she can get notice of cancellation of the insurance. In these new tenancies, landlords may charge up to $50 per violation of a written pet agreement or facility pet rules.

After a rule change, any notice terminating tenancy for violation of the rule must include a statement that the tenant may, within seven days, make a written request for resolution through the facility's informal dispute resolution process. If the tenant serves such a request, the landlord may not file an eviction action until 30 days after the tenant's request or the completion of the informal dispute resolution process, whichever occurs first. There is no requirement that the parties agree to any result through this process; if they cannot agree, the next step is an eviction action.

Note also that the statute requires a termination notice to refer to the facility's informal dispute resolution process only when the notice is based on violation of a changed rule. Although a facility dispute resolution process or rental agreement may provide for such language in termination notices based on violations of rules the landlord has not changed (or any other violation), the statutes do not require this.

In a facility-wide election, tenants may elect one committee of up to seven members to make a written request to the landlord for a meeting to discuss issues other than rent, up to two times per year (ORS 90.600). The landlord or landlord's representative must meet with the group within 10 to 30 days of its request. After the meeting, the committee must send a summary of the discussion to the landlord, to which the landlord has a duty to make a good faith response within 60 days. The tenants' committee has recourse to informal dispute resolution if the landlord fails to meet with the group or to respond in good faith to the written summary.

Chapter Fourteen

HOUSING DISCRIMINATION LAWS AND OTHER LAWS AFFECTING LANDLORD-TENANT RIGHTS

1. Housing Discrimination

Both landlords and tenants need to know about laws prohibiting discrimination. For landlords, this knowledge is essential to making fair decisions and avoiding liability. For tenants, knowledge of the law can be the key that unlocks safe and decent housing otherwise closed to them.

Government-funded agencies that subsidize tenant rents, rental-management companies, and public housing authorities also must abide by fair housing laws. Some typical problems tenants encounter with these organizations are described below.

1.1 Who is protected

A range of laws — federal, state, and even local — protects tenants and prospective tenants from discrimination. The oldest is the Civil Rights Act of 1866, which prohibits racial discrimination. More recently, the Fair Housing Act of 1968 banned discrimination on the grounds of race, color, religion, sex, and national origin. The newest federal protection came in the Fair

Housing Act Amendments of 1988, which added handicap and "familial status" (having children).

Under this law, "handicap" has three meanings: (1) a physical or mental impairment that substantially limits a major life activity; (2) having a history of such an impairment; or (3) being regarded as having such an impairment, even if there is no actual impairment. Alcoholism is considered an impairment, but improper behavior by a person who is alcohol-dependent is viewed as conduct, not impairment. AIDS and HIV infection are considered impairments. The law permits landlords to refuse to rent or to continue to rent to those who use or are addicted to illegal drugs. Landlords do not have to rent to people who have been convicted of illegal manufacture or distribution of drugs. They do not have to rent to an impaired person whose tenancy would constitute a direct threat to health or safety or a threat of substantial harm to property.

"Familial status" under this law requires landlords not only to accept new tenants with children younger than 18 years old, but also to make sure that rules and regulations at the rental housing do not unfairly burden families with children. Landlords cannot use the pregnancy of a tenant or the birth or adoption of a child as a basis for eviction. Nor can the landlord charge the tenant different fees because the tenant has children. A parent who designates someone else — such as grandparents — to care full-time for a child can do so without subjecting the grandparents to eviction. Parents who have visitation time with their children but not full-time custody also are entitled to protection under this law.

There is one exception to the requirement to rent to people with children — housing designated for older persons. Children can be barred from some complexes where housing is publicly funded for seniors; all tenants are 62 or older; or at least 80 percent of the households in the complex are headed by someone 55 or older and the complex has published rules that show its intent to limit housing to those 55 or older. Because "senior" complexes are sometimes subject to federal regulations that define "family" broadly, some elders in these complexes may be able to have young family members living with them. Legal advice can be crucial.

1.2 Kinds of discrimination

Federal and state law both recognize two kinds of discrimination — deliberate unfair treatment of an individual based on improper criteria ("discriminatory treatment"), and the use of policies that may seem neutral but have the effect of targeting people based on improper criteria ("disparate impact"). An example of disparate impact under federal law is a requirement that no more than two persons may use one bedroom under any circumstances, since that rule might have the effect of keeping out families with children. An example under Oregon law would be a requirement that all tenants be at least six feet tall — thus having the effect of barring women.

1.3   State and local anti-discrimination laws

State law prohibits the same kinds of housing discrimination the federal laws do, and more — discrimination based on one's source of income, marital status, or one's status as a victim of domestic violence, stalking, or sexual assault crimes all are unlawful in Oregon. Landlords cannot bar tenants who have won an eviction case on the merits against an earlier landlord. In addition, a landlord may not deny housing to someone who has a guide dog or other "assistance animals," even if the landlord otherwise prohibits pets. On farms and nurseries that have worker housing, an attempt at retaliatory eviction of workers who seek legal advice about their rights or who attempt to unionize can violate not only the workers' labor rights but also constitute discrimination if the affected workers are all of one race or ethnic origin (see ORS 659A.259).

At least a few local governments also have ordinances protecting certain groups from housing discrimination. Multnomah County, Portland, Salem, Eugene, and Corvallis protect tenants from discrimination based on sexual orientation, age, and gender identity; Ashland protects tenants from sexual orientation discrimination. From time to time local ordinances may change; landlords and tenants should inquire of their city and county governments about which kinds of discrimination are unlawful.

1.4   Avoiding discrimination

Landlords who discriminate unlawfully may find themselves in state or federal court facing injunctions and hefty damages, including punitive damages in some cases. Illegal discrimination makes bad business sense.

What can conscientious landlords do to avoid claims of discrimination? Numerous landlord and fair housing organizations offer assistance and training; some of them are listed in chapter 15. One landlord lobbyist summed up the answer nicely: "Do a criminal background check and a credit check on the prospective tenant. Know how much money a tenant needs to have to rent the unit and pay for related expenses such as utilities, cable, and parking; and decide how much of a credit risk you want to take. Write down your objective criteria. Then rent the place to the first applicant who meets those criteria. Every time."

It is helpful to break down the process into steps. First, advertising a unit should not specify or suggest who should think about living there: "perfect for married couple" or "women only" may be invitations to a lawsuit. Second, use background checks prudently, limiting your criteria to a person's past rental history, credit rating, and criminal history. Looking into a person's religious background, national origin, or sexual orientation isn't reasonably related to the person's future reliability as a tenant. Remember, every prospective tenant should be judged according to the same criteria.

When selecting a tenant, the landlord should charge the same fees and deposits that other tenants would be expected to pay. (**Note:** A landlord cannot charge a deposit for a person with disabilities to modify a unit to make it usable.) The landlord should not "steer" people of one race or ethnic background to one complex or part of a complex, nor refuse to make repairs to units occupied by tenants in a protected category. The landlord should not restrict families with children to certain units or floors, either.

The landlord should apply the same rules to all tenants — including children. Rules should reasonably limit activity for the health and safety of all tenants.

Occupancy limits can have the effect of discriminating against families with children or families of ethnic backgrounds in which large extended families are the norm. Oregon law says that two persons per bedroom is an acceptable minimum, but the key word is "minimum" (ORS 90.262). This number may be unreasonably restrictive when the circumstances are viewed as a whole — the size of the bedrooms, the overall size of the rental, the ages of children.

Landlords may not discriminate lawfully against persons who do not speak English. However, it is the tenants' responsibility to arrange for interpreters or translators as needed to communicate with the landlord.

Tenants have the protection of fair housing laws even if they are not citizens. Landlords should know, too, that it is unlawful to discriminate against a tenant's friends or visitors because of race, marital status, ethnic background, etc.

A landlord who demands sexual favors from tenants can be subject to a claim of sexual harassment, which is a form of sex discrimination.

Landlords can avoid some claims of discrimination on the basis of disability by making sure their rental application forms and all subsequent notices ask the tenant whether the tenant has a disability for which the tenant seeks special accommodation. It is up to the tenant to notify the landlord of the need for accomodation, and to suggest what that accommodation should be. The landlord can demand verification of the disability. If the tenant's request is reasonable, the landlord can refuse to accommodate only if granting the request would create an undue burden or somehow change the nature of the parties' relationship.

The law specifically provides that tenants with disabilities can modify a rental unit to make it usable for themselves. They must do so at their own expense, however, unless their landlord is a public agency. If the modification would limit the usability of the rental by other tenants later, the tenant is responsible for removing the modification at the end of the tenancy. Although tenants in this situation can be required to open an escrow account to cover the cost of restoring the unit to its previous condition, the landlord cannot charge them a deposit in addition to the escrow account. Applicants and tenants with mental health disabilities are entitled to reasonable accommodations in the landlord's housing rules.

Landlords need to know that all new residential projects of four or more units — "new" meaning complexes built after January 12, 1990 — must have units that are handicap-accessible and adaptable to wheelchair use. Knobs, faucets, and switches must be reachable, walls must be reinforced for grab bars. Most building contractors are familiar with the specific requirements, as are housing assistance agencies.

The 2003 legislature created protections for tenants who are recent victims of sexual assault, stalking, and domestic violence crimes. If given proper written notice, landlords must allow such victims, on showing documentation of the crime, to terminate rental agreements early, or, if asked, change locks at the victim's expense and exclude a tenant perpetrator living in the same unit without court process. Landlords may not evict the crime victims, nor increase fees or deposits, based on their status as crime victims.

Finally, landlords must keep in mind that all tenants have the right to the peaceful enjoyment of their homes. If a landlord learns that a tenant is harassing or threatening another tenant because of that person's race, national origin, or other grounds for unlawful discrimination, it is the landlord's duty to intervene, doing what is necessary to stop the harassment — including evicting the harasser.

1.5 Tenant remedies

While law-abiding landlords do their best to ensure fair housing opportunities, there are unfortunately many cases in which tenants still face hurtful discrimination. What tenants can do to combat the discrimination depends on which laws have been violated and how easily and quickly the tenant can find legal help.

If a tenant has reason to believe a landlord has discriminated in violation of the Fair Housing Act and its amendments, the tenant has three options — file an agency complaint with the Department of Housing and Urban Development (HUD) or the Civil Rights Division of Oregon's Bureau of Labor and Industries (BOLI), or go directly to court. If it appears that the landlord has violated only state or local antidiscrimination laws, the tenant can file a complaint only with BOLI or start a court case.

What the tenant decides to do will be based in part on what has happened: has the tenant been denied access to housing? Is the landlord making unfair rules or applying them unfairly? Is the landlord attempting to evict the tenant for unlawfully discriminatory reasons? The administrative agency process may be able to provide a thorough investigation at no cost to the tenant, but the process takes time. The agencies begin with fact-finding and generally offer to mediate complaints. Even in mediation, it is possible for a wronged tenant to obtain payment for the harm done and an agreement by a landlord not to continue the unlawful conduct. If mediation does not work, the next step may be a formal administrative hearing. Regrettably, the agencies are understaffed and cannot always investigate promptly or well. The tenant can opt to transfer the case to court or start directly in court, where it is possible to get a restraining order against the landlord to stop the unlawful behavior, and a permanent injunction that might require the landlord to make the next vacant unit available. The tenant may be awarded money for damages and even punitive damages if the case is particularly offensive.

Regardless of how the tenant chooses to proceed, it is important to have as much evidence of the discrimination as possible. An excellent, and free, way to get this kind of evidence is through "testing" performed by the Fair Housing Council of Oregon (see chapter 15 for a description of this service). The tenant should contact the Housing Council right away, even if he or she has not yet decided what to do about the discrimination. The Housing Council may be able to help find a knowledgeable lawyer to handle the tenant's case. In exceptional cases, the Housing Council itself may start a lawsuit.

Oregon's landlord-tenant act makes it unlawful for a landlord to discriminate unlawfully against a tenant in violation of federal, state, or local law. A tenant who can prove a violation has a defense (meaning that the tenant can win in court) in any discriminatory case brought against the tenant by the landlord, so long as the tenant does not owe any back rent. Even if a tenant is in default, though, there may be circumstances that show discrimination. An example is a housing complex where most of the tenants work seasonally. None of them is able to pay rent during the winter months, but the landlord evicts the Hispanic tenants for nonpayment while relaxing the rules for everyone else. Even when this law does not protect tenants who owe rent, the other laws described above can provide those tenants with a defense against a landlord's case against them regardless of the status of the tenants' rent. Furthermore, even in an eviction case that itself is not discriminatory, tenants can file a counterclaim for unlawful discrimination that arose at another time.

Housing authorities and other helping agencies may behave discriminatorily as well. The following are examples of discrimination that could occur by a housing authority or other agency: they may move names on waiting lists for apartments; or try to put all families with children, or all persons of the same race, in one part of a complex; or refuse to make reasonable accommodations for people with disabilities; or provide opportunities for vouchers or rent supplements in a way that favors certain categories of people arbitrarily. Applicants for and tenants of subsidized housing should get legal advice about their rights in these situations.

There are time limits by which tenants or applicants for housing must raise any complaint of discrimination. The deadlines vary from law to law; getting prompt legal advice can help prevent the loss of rights. When an eviction is pending, it is especially crucial to get help in a hurry.

2. Other Laws

Tenants have some protections against improper landlord conduct under Oregon's Unlawful Debt Collection Practices Act (UDCPA) and its Unlawful Trade Practices Act (UTPA). These protections arise when the landlord's conduct is improper under those laws but when the conduct is not covered by ORLTA. The UDCPA makes the following kinds of conduct unlawful when they are for the purpose of getting a tenant to pay rent or other debts:

- Using threat of force or violence against tenant or tenant's property

- Threatening arrest or criminal prosecution for nonpayment

- Threatening to seize or sell tenant's belongings without court order

- Using profane, obscene, or abusive language

- Repeated contact with tenant or contact at times known to be inconvenient, so as to harass or annoy members of tenant's family

- Contacting or threatening to contact tenant's employer about existence or nature of debt

- Telephoning tenant at work when tenant has not given permission for such calls or when employer is known not to permit such calls, or telephoning more than one time per week when calls at work are permitted and if landlord has been unsuccessful in reaching tenant at home either during daytime or evening hours before 9 p.m.

- Writing to tenant about the debt without telling tenant who is writing or how to reach the writer

- Failing to identify caller and purpose of call within 30 seconds

- Causing any expense to tenant by concealing true purpose of communication (e.g., long distance telephone charges)

- Attempting or threatening to enforce a right or remedy when knowing the right or remedy does not exist or when such enforcement activity is not within collector's regular course of business

- Using any form of contact that simulates legal process or pretends government authorization

- Claiming fees and charges can be added when they cannot

- Attempting to collect interest not permitted by law nor by the contract the parties have signed

- Threatening to turn over tenant's account to abusive collector or inferring that tenant will lose defenses if the account is turned over to a collector (ORS 646.639).

A tenant who wins a claim in court based on UDCPA may be awarded damages of up to $200; obtain an injunction; or be awarded punitive damages if the conduct is exceptionally improper. The winner in such a case is entitled to have his or her attorney fees and court costs paid by the losing party (ORS 646.641).

The UTPA provides the same remedies, but for a different range of unlawful practices (ORS 646.608, ORS 646.638); these include the following:

- Falsely claiming real estate belongs to someone else; that real estate has qualities, characteristics, or uses, or benefits it does not have (e.g., "swim in the warm ocean waters at your new home on Oregon's sunny coast") or standards it does not meet; or that real estate is new if it is deteriorated or has been altered

- Advertising real estate with the intent not to provide it as advertised, or within the time period promised

- Giving false reasons for existence of, reasons for, or amount of price reductions

- Giving false or misleading information about the landlord's cost for real estate or services

- Failing to disclose any known material defect at the time of turning over the real estate to the tenant

In some kinds of UTPA cases, only the attorney general, and not private individuals, can enforce compliance. These cases involve "unconscionable tactics," such as knowingly taking advantage of a tenant's illiteracy or letting a very low-income person enter into a rental agreement when there is no reasonable probability the tenant can pay the rent in full when due (ORS 646.607).

A tenant who is being evicted and who has claims under either of these two laws can raise the violations as counterclaims; otherwise, these claims can be pursued separately in a small claims action.

CHAPTER FIFTEEN

GETTING ASSISTANCE

Once you have read this book, you are likely to know more about landlord-tenant law than some Oregon attorneys. Still, the law at every level is always changing, and in Oregon, landlord-tenant law is becoming increasingly complex. If you find your situation going from bad to worse, the time to look for legal help is now. A lawyer is trained to know how to gauge situations objectively, understand proper procedure, and negotiate effectively.

1. Finding an Attorney

Landlords have some distinct advantages over tenants when it comes to finding a lawyer. First, they are much more likely to be able to pay for legal assistance. Second, they have access to various landlord associations (see section 4. below) that can recommend lawyers who routinely represent landlords. And third, if the case involves an attempt to evict the tenant, putting on a defense for the tenant is usually more involved than the landlord's side of the case, so it will likely be more costly for the tenant to win the case. Although ORLTA provides for the losing party to pay for the winning party's attorney fees and court costs (ORS 90.255) the possibility of getting paid later is not much incentive for most attorneys to take a case without some payment first.

The Oregon State Bar offers two basic resources for both landlords and tenants. The first is the statewide Lawyer Referral Service, which offers initial consultations with local lawyers who accept this kind of case for no more than $35. The second program is the Modest Means Panel for lower-income persons. This program provides reduced fee services beginning at $35 for an initial consultation and then at no more than $60 per hour for continuing representation. You can contact either program by calling 503-684-3763 (Portland) or 1-800-452-7636 (statewide) and asking for a referral for one of the programs.

Another resource for both landlords and tenants is the local telephone directory, which lists lawyers by the kind of work they do. Some listings for real-estate lawyers say they accept this kind of case, and may even say which side they represent. A tenant who calls one of these lawyers should find out whether the lawyer usually works with landlords, as such a lawyer may not be familiar with tenant defenses and strategies.

A third resource is courthouse files, which are public records, of landlord-tenant cases that have gone through the courts. Which lawyers appear most frequently? Which side do they represent? How often do they win cases compared to other lawyers on the same side of similar cases?

A final resource is the Oregon State Bar's disciplinary complaints office. Unlike other states, Oregon keeps records of complaints about attorneys open to the public. Anyone can call the bar complaints unit to find out about an attorney's history. The telephone numbers are 503-620-0222 (Portland area) or 1-800-452-8260 (statewide).

Some very low-income tenants may be able to get help free from local legal aid offices. The lawyers in these programs tend to be very familiar with eviction defenses, rights of tenant unions, and subsidized housing law. These programs do not have enough staff to handle all cases. Some of them coordinate volunteer-lawyer panels to help additional low-income tenants. The Northwestern School of Law, in Portland, has a clinic that may be able to help some low-income tenants with eviction hearings (telephone number: 503-768-6500).

Some landlords' associations offer legal-information "hotlines" for their members faced with problems. A similar hotline for tenants exists at the Washington County community action agency's Housing Advocacy Group; another is at the Community

Alliance of Tenants, in Portland, and it's called the Renter's Rights Hotline (telephone number: 503-288-0130).

Landlords and tenants have access to free recorded information from the State Bar's Tel-Law program, with selections about notices, eviction causes and defenses, abandoned belongings, privacy rights, and more. More information regarding Tel-Law is available online at <www.osbar.org>.

2. Legislative Lobbying and Tenants' Unions

Almost all landlord-tenant law is made at the state level. Landlord groups are well represented by lobbyists in Salem; the process is harder for tenants. Tenants can try to influence legislators individually, but concerted action is usually more effective. Some tenants' organizations are active in the legislature, as described below.

Even tenants who have no access to a lobbyist may have had experiences or concerns that would be important for lawmakers to hear when they are considering bills in the future. Tenants who have had problems they think merit legislative attention should telephone the Oregon Law Center at 503-295-2760.

Tenants' unions may or may not be concerned with state law. Typically, a tenants' union is organized on a neighborhood, city, or other geographical basis, or around problems with a landlord they have in common. The objectives of a tenants' union may be to improve tenants' rights generally through legislation or regulations, or to use combined economic power to demand collective bargaining from a landlord. A tenants' union is likely to be the most effective means of enforcing any tenants' rights, and most of the remedies discussed in this book may be used by tenants working together. This kind of organization is likely to seek such goals as —

- freedom from arbitrary no-cause evictions,

- tenant participation in rule-making,

- limitations on rent increases, and

- repairs.

Landlords may not lawfully retaliate against tenants who join together to protect their rights (ORS 90.385 and ORS 90.750).

Subject to the limitations discussed in chapter 8, a landlord should not win an eviction case if the tenant establishes that the motive for the eviction was to retaliate against the tenant for tenants' union activities.

Tenants in HUD-subsidized housing can get help building a union from a nationwide group called the National Alliance of HUD Tenants in Boston, Massachusetts, at 617-267-9564. Public housing and private tenants alike can get more information about tenants' unions from the Community Alliance of Tenants Renter's Rights Hotline, in Portland (503-288-0130), or the Oregon Law Center, also in Portland (503-295-2760).

Getting help from a lawyer in establishing a tenants' union can be important, although it is the members themselves who should define and decide the group's direction and purpose. Besides, lawyers are inherently conservative — they are trained to foresee the worst possible outcomes and to avoid them as completely as possible. Ask your organization's lawyer about the risks, but make sure he or she doesn't take part in deciding whether those risks are worth taking.

3. Help in Paying the Rent

Tenants may find that an emergency has made it impossible for them to pay all or even some of the rent they owe. In some situations, they may be eligible for small amounts of temporary assistance from local governments, community action agencies, church organizations, the Red Cross, groups affiliated with some housing authorities, or Oregon's Children and Families Division (CAF). CAF can be especially helpful to families who need to move in order to escape from domestic violence. **Note:** Legal aid offices do not have funds to give or lend to needy tenants.

Seniors with limited incomes may qualify for the Oregon Elderly Rental Assistance Program. This assistance, which takes the form of an annual payment, is available if —

- you are 58 or older by the end of the year immediately preceding the year in which assistance is claimed,

- your annual income is less than $10,000,

- your total rent for the year (not including deposits) plus fuel and utility payments (except for telephone bills) is more than 20 percent of your household income, and

- you file an appropriate claim with the Department of Revenue.

- The amount of the rental assistance payment could be as much as $250, depending on the amount of your income and your rent. You must file a claim each year for this payment. Contact the Oregon Department of Revenue for more information on the Elderly Rental Assistance program.

4. Landlords' Organizations

A number of organizations represent the interests of landlords. The longest-established is the Multifamily Housing Council of Oregon, which represents a wide range of landlords and offers education, tenant screening, state and local legislative advocacy, forms, landlord hotline, and other assistance (telephone 503-378-1912; statewide 1-800-378-7129; or Web site <www.mfhco.com>).

The Oregon Rental Housing Association is an umbrella association in Salem with over a dozen local affiliates, offering education, legislative advocacy, forms, and other assistance (telephone 503-364-5468 or Web site <www.oregonrentalhousing.com>). There are several local landlord organizations as well, such as Metro Multi-Family Housing Association, in Portland (telephone 503-226-4533), and specialty groups such as the Institute of Real Estate Managers.

Intrepid landlords can browse the Internet on more than 200,000 Web sites for information and forms. Many of them offer nationwide forms and other services that may be too general to be practical. Remember, every state's landlord-tenant law is different, so relying on information from sources at the state level seems far less risky for the most part.

5. Mobile (Manufactured) Home Resources

The primary interest group for owners of manufactured housing who rent space in parks or facilities is Manufactured Home Owners of Oregon, in Salem (503-393-7737). Manufactured Housing Communities of Oregon (MHCO), also in Salem, represents landlords of mobile home/manufactured housing facilities (503-391-4496).

Oregon's Housing and Community Services Department provides limited assistance, including dispute resolution, to tenants and landlords through its Office of Manufactured Dwelling Park Community Relations (503-986-2000).

6. Legal Aid Programs

Lack of funding and government-imposed restrictions on services has made finding a legal aid lawyer more difficult, but Oregon still has several programs that low-income tenants can contact. The largest is Legal Aid Services of Oregon (LASO), with offices that serve several counties, located in the following areas:

- Albany (541-926-8679)

- Bend (541-385-6944)

- Hillsboro (503-648-7163)

- Newport (541-265-5305)

- Oregon City (503-655-2518)

- Pendleton (541-276-6685)

- Portland (503-224-4086)

- Roseburg (541-673-1181)

Lane County has Lane County Legal Aid and Lane County Law and Advocacy Center, both reachable at 541-342-6056. Marion-Polk Legal Aid Service serves two counties (503-581-5265). The Center for Nonprofit Legal Services in Medford serves Jackson County (541-779-7292).

The second largest organization is the Oregon Law Center (OLC), with offices that serve several counties located in the following areas:

- Coos Bay (541-269-1226)

- Grants Pass (541-476-1058)

- Ontario (541-889-3121)

- Portland (503 295 2760)

- Woodburn (503-981-0373)

Oregon's legal aid programs have a Web site that discusses many of the rights of residential tenants. The site also indicates which LASO and OLC offices currently serve the various counties (see <www.oregonlawhelp.org>).

Seniors aged 60 or older may be able to get help through volunteer attorneys at local senior centers as well as through some legal aid offices. In some locations, AARP members can get a free 30-minute consultation with local attorneys.

7. Fair Housing (Anti-discrimination) Resources

Chapter 14 introduced the Fair Housing Council of Oregon (503-223-8295 in Portland; 1-800-424-3247 statewide; Web site <www.fhco.org>), a valuable resource for landlords, tenants, and housing applicants. The Fair Housing Council offers state-law and federal-law fair-housing training for landlord groups. For housing applicants and some tenants (and the occasional owner who wants to make sure managers are following the law), it conducts testing by using mock applicants or tenants as a tool to investigate unlawfully discriminatory practices. Trained testers present themselves as similar to actual applicants applying for housing when real applicants believe they have been rejected or discouraged from housing opportunities because of their race, sex, national origin, family status, or other federal or state-protected category. The Council works with legal aid programs and private attorneys in providing enforcement referrals and resources. It also refers cases to the federal Department of Housing and Urban Development (HUD) and to the Civil Rights Division of the Oregon Bureau of Labor and Industries. To contact HUD, call 1-800-877-741-3281 or go to the Web site at <www.hud.gov>. The Civil Rights Division can be contacted in the following areas:

- Eugene (541-686-7623)
- Medford (541-776-6197)
- Pendleton (541-276-7884)
- Portland (503-731-4075)

Local communities with ordinances that protect additional categories of people may have their own testing and enforcement services. For example, Lane County has a Community Housing Resource Board, which sponsors the Southern Oregon Fair Housing Project. Contact city and county governments to determine what kind of enforcement they offer in your area.

For people with disabilities, there is one more resource, the Oregon Advocacy Center in Portland, whose staff includes attorneys and reasonable accommodation specialists. To reach the Oregon Advocacy Center, call 503-243-2081.

APPENDIX
....

ELEMENTS OF A
RESIDENTIAL EVICTION

ELEMENTS OF A RESIDENTIAL EVICTION

Landlord Issues Eviction Notice

types	ORS 90.427
	ORS 90.400
	ORS 90.632*
service	ORS 90.155,
	ORS 90.400,
	ORS 90.405,
	ORS 90.632*
validity	ORS 105.115,
	ORS 105.120

Landlord Files Complaint

filing	ORS 105.110
service	ORS 105.135

7 JUDICIAL DAYS

First Appearance

date	ORS 105.130
failure to appear	ORS 105.137
motion to dismiss	
invalid notice	ORS 105.115,
	ORS 105.120,
	ORS 90.400
	ORS 90.429*
	ORS 90.630*
answer	ORS 105.137
amending answer	ORS 105.137

TRIAL

"as soon as practicable" within	
15 days	ORS 105.137
abatement	ORS 105.138*
continuance	ORS 105.140

DEFENSES

defective notice	
cure:	
tender	ORS 81.020
	ORS 90.140
good cause	ORS 90.400,
	ORS 90.405
	ORS 90.630*
prepaid rent	ORS 105.120
waiver, estoppel	ORS 90.415
bad faith	ORS 90.130
unconscionability	ORS 90.245
real party in	
interest	ORS 105.130
statute of	
limitations	ORS 12.125
unenforceable	
rule	ORS 90.262
unreasonable	
conditions of	ORS 90.525
rental	ORS 90.375,
retaliation	ORS 90.385,
	ORS 90.765*
discrimination	ORS 90.390
breach not	
material/	ORS 90.400
outrageous	ORS 90.630*

Counterclaims

habitability	ORS 90.360
essential services	ORS 90.365
substitute housing	ORS 90.365
retaliation	ORS 90.375
	ORS 90.385
	ORS 90.765*
conversion	ORS 90.425
lockout	ORS 90.375
utility shutoff	ORS 90.375
abuse of access	ORS 90.322
unlawful debt	
collection	ORS 646.649
unlawful trade	
practices	ORS 646.607,
	ORS 646.608
prohibited	ORS 90.245,
provisions	ORS 90.750*
	ORS 90.755*
nondisclosure	ORS 90.315
discrimination	ORS Ch 659A

Judgment

restitution	ORS 105.145
delay	ORS 105.148
dismissal	ORS 105.145
stay	ORS 90.475

Execution of Judgment

ORS 105.151

Appeal to Court of Appeals**

within 30 days	
from judgment	ORS 19.225
expedited appeal,	ORS 19.335
stay of execution	ORAP 7.35,
	ORAP 7.40

Disposal of Tenant Belongings

ORS 105.165
ORS 90.425
ORS 90.975*

*manufacured home and moorage space rentals in facilities only

**excluding appeals from justice court — ORS ch 34

OTHER TITLES IN THE SELF-COUNSEL SERIES

Simply Essential Landlord's Kit
Timothy Madden
$11.95
ISBN 1-55180-384-4

- Have the information you need at your fingertips

- Learn how to document all landlord/tenant agreements

- Track your revenue and stay organized

Being a landlord just got easier! The *Simply Essential Landlord's Kit* is the best thing to come along since postdated checks. The dozens of forms included cover every aspect of building and tenancy management. Whether you're a landlord of only one small apartment or of a whole building, a superintendent, a caretaker, or a maintenance worker, this kit will help you stay organized and profitable.

Simply Essential Home Moving Kit
Richard Stephens
$11.95
ISBN 1-55180-369-0

- Prepare your family for moving day

- Avoid costly mistakes

- Stay organized

Moving house can be a great source of stress on you and your relationship. The *Simply Essential Home Moving Kit* will help you orchestrate this seemingly impossible task in an organized and timely manner. It deals with neighborhood-to-neighborhood, city-to-city, and country-to-country moves, and contains information and checklists that will ensure a smooth move with little hassle. This kit is also packed with useful tips for minimizing damage to property and keeping your move on schedule. Worksheets and checklists are included on paper and on disk.

Simply Essential Disaster Preparation Kit

Catherine Stuart
$11.95
ISBN 1-55180-385-2

- Learn how to prepare for the unexpected — from floods to earthquakes

- Understand life-saving procedures

- Protect your family, possessions, and pets

The power's out, the heat's off, the lines of communication are down. It will be days before rescue and clean-up crews can restore order to your community. In the meantime, you need to find edible food, clean water, and maybe even medical supplies. Could you do it?

You can if you're properly prepared. The *Simply Essential Disaster Planning Kit* is designed to give individuals and families the information they need to prepare for, mitigate, and increase their chances of surviving a major disaster.

Order Form

Name _____

Address_____

_____

_____

Charge to: ☐ Visa ☐ MasterCard

Account Number_____

Validation Date _____

Expiry Date _____

Signature _____

Shipping and handling will apply.

In Washington, 7.8% sales tax will be added.

Yes, please send me the following:

____ *Simply Essential Landlord's Kit*

____ *Simply Essential Home Moving Kit*

____ *Simply Essential Disaster Preparation Kit*

Please add $5.95 for postage and handling.

☐ Check here for a free catalog

Self-Counsel Press, Inc.
1704 N. State Street
Bellingham, WA 98225

Visit our Web site:
www.self-counsel.com